Held In Trust

For everyone, forever.

The Properties and Collections of
the Bermuda National Trust

© 2008 Bermuda National Trust
PO Box HM 61
Hamilton HM AX
Bermuda
Tel: (441) 236-6483
Fax: (441) 236-0617
E-mail: Palmetto@bnt.bm
Website: www.bnt.bm

ISBN 978-1-897403-63-1
Design and Production by Dace McCoy Ground
Printed in Hong Kong

This book is dedicated to the many people who have held, continue to hold and will hold the care and protection of Bermuda's unique heritage in their hands.

First, there were those individuals who started the Bermuda Historical Monuments Trust in 1937; a prescient group who saw the future and the risks it held for our natural and man-made heritage, and took action. Then came the Bermuda National Trust with its tireless teams of workers, volunteers and members; often against all odds, they have assembled a remarkable array of things Bermudian for all to enjoy and appreciate. The Trust continues to care for these and educate the community on their value to us as a people. Finally, a special dedication to future generations who will soon have the responsibility for their fine heritage; we hope they will prize it as those before them have.

This book, a portfolio of the Bermudian heritage held by the National Trust in care for everyone forever, is dedicated to all of you: past, present and future.

Contributors

This project was carried out by a committee of four, all of whom contributed to every aspect of the book in addition to their particular areas of concentration:

◇ Dace McCoy Ground wrote the main text, designed the book and laid it out.
◇ Margaret Lloyd researched the deeds and history of the properties, served as the 'fact editor' and wrote the introduction to the Historic Properties chapter.
◇ Amanda Outerbridge edited the text.
◇ Katherine Cooper Berry did initial research, consulted on the design and took all the pictures in the Historic Properties and Cemeteries chapters and all other pictures with the 'KCB' photo credit.

Other contributors:

◇ William Zuill wrote up his memories of the early days of the Trust and supplemented the research with his detailed knowledge.
◇ Richard Ground took all the pictures in the Collections chapter and all other pictures with the 'RWG' photo credit.
◇ Hilary Tulloch, David Wingate and Hugh Davidson wrote the introductions to the Cemeteries, Protected Open Space and Collections chapters respectively.
◇ Richard Lowry wrote the sidebar on the Archaeological Research Committee.
◇ Diana Chudleigh and Hilary Tulloch proofread the book; Steve Conway and Connie Dey reviewed the text.
◇ The Trust staff – particularly Laura Lyons – helped at every stage.
◇ The Historic Properties chapter draws mostly from the Trust's Architectural Heritage book series and the research done by a team of volunteer researchers, many of whom have been working on the project for 15 years. Interested readers should go to the original books for fuller coverage of the properties and their histories.
◇ The Cemeteries chapter is drawn from Hilary and Richard Tulloch's meticulous research and their report, soon to be book, *Died at Bermuda*.
◇ The Collections chapter draws heavily from the first publication of the Bermuda National Trust, Bryden B Hyde's *Bermuda's Antique Furniture & Silver*, and from the great depth of knowledge of the Trust's long-time chairman of the Museums Committee, Hugh Davidson.
◇ The Protected Open Space chapter is drawn from David Wingate's detailed environmental assessments of Trust reserves.

This book is a compilation of the research and writing done by many
Trust volunteers over the years. Every one of these people has given
freely of both time and skill to help make the Bermuda National Trust
what it is today. We celebrate them all.

Table of Contents

Preface 1
Foreword to the First Edition 2
How it All Began 3
The Bermuda Historical
      Monuments Trust 5

CHAPTER 1
Historic Properties 7
Buckingham 8
The Casino 10
Bridge House 12
Reeve Court 14
President Henry Tucker House 16
Stewart Hall 20
Samaritans' Lodge 22
Samaritans' Cottages 24
The Globe Hotel 26
The Old Rectory 28
Fanny Fox's Cottage 30
The Unfinished Church 32
Verdmont 34
Palmetto House 38
School Lands Cottage 40
Pembroke Hall 42
Waterville and Waterville Park 44
Belair 48
Ship's Inn 50
Cluster Cottage 52
Tivoli 54
Springfield 56
The Keep at Royal Naval
      Dockyard 58

Sidebar: The Architectural
Heritage Project 60

CHAPTER 2
Historic Cemeteries 61
Garrison 62
St George's Military 62
Yellow Fever 64
Hayward Burial Ground 64
Nonsuch Island 66
Jennings Land Burial Ground 66
Garrison Cemetery Prospect 66
Long Island 68
Ports Island 68
Somerset Island Military 70
Convict 70
Royal Naval 72
Watford 72

Sidebar: Dr David Wingate 74

CHAPTER 3
Protected Open Space 75
Central Wetlands 76
HT North 76
JMH Cooper 78
Spittal Pond Bird Sanctuary 78
Gibbons 82
Devonshire Marsh 82
Paget Marsh 84
Warwick Pond and Powell
      Woodland 88
Higgs 88
Woodland Nature Reserves 90
Wilkinson 88
IW Hughes 88
Butterfield 90
Middleton and S-Hill 92
Elm Lodge 94

Chaplin O'Neill 94
Tivoli North 96
Lighthouse Hill 96
Scaur Lodge 98
Gladys Morrell 98
Gilbert 100
Coastline and Islands 102
Smith's Island 102
Bee Hive Farm 102
Rogue Island 104
Saltus Island 104
Buck Island 104
Marjorie Jackson 106
Morgan and Palm Islands 106
Farmlands 108
Stokes Point Farm 108
Locust Hall Farm 110
Paget Marsh Farmland and
      Lammermuir Cottage 110
Other Trust Farmlands 110
Buy Back Bermuda 112
Somerset Long Bay East 112
Buy Back Bermuda Phase II 114

Sidebar: The Archaeological
Research Committee 116

CHAPTER 4
Collections 117
The Bermuda Archives 118
Paintings and Artwork 120
Furniture 124
Silver 126
Porcelain and Pottery 130
Other Elements 132

Index 134

Preface

This new edition of *Held In Trust* provides a comprehensive account of the buildings, land and artefacts under the stewardship of the Bermuda National Trust. It is a record of a priceless national legacy that has taken over 70 years and the devoted efforts of thousands of individuals and organisations to create. When one considers the effort required in acquiring just one iconic building or green oasis the achievement evident in this volume is staggering.

It is especially poignant to revisit and update the holdings of the Trust in 2008, almost 20 years since the first edition of this work. While we are immensely proud of what has been achieved in that interval we are all too aware of the countless buildings and open spaces that have been lost forever that we would have dearly loved to have been able to include in this book. It has also emphatically illustrated just how large a piece of Bermuda's cultural and environmental heritage is in the care of the Trust.

To members and friends whose generosity and involvement allows the vital work of the Trust to continue and expand, we hope you are pleased by all that has been accomplished. To those who may be seeing the depth and commitment of the Trust to both Bermuda's past and future for the first time, please join us; we could use your help.

It is our hope that each reader who explores the treasures of the Trust in these pages will be inspired to experience them in person.

Bill Holmes
President of the Trust Council

July 2008

Foreword to the First Edition

Separated by time and space from the mainstream of continental development the islands of the world have evolved as tiny microcosms unto themselves. Their separateness and their age "the particular climatic conditions, the diversity of geological origins and the absence of large predators have allowed the evolution of a myriad of indigenous laboratories and multiplied the opportunities for life. Needing to adapt themselves to a special environment, insular fauna and flora have developed a systematic peculiarity transforming their mini-habitat into a unique and therefore priceless microcosm. Furthermore, within their delicate environmental balance, they must live with the insidious corrosion of salt air and the unremitting erosion by the sea. Different in degree, not in kind, the islands of the world are like the pearls of a necklace, and they encircle the globe — a ribbon of delicate and irreplaceable gems."*

One of these irreplaceable gems, Bermuda, sits alone out in the mid-Atlantic, the coral cap of an extinct volcano. Through aeons of isolation, the island developed birds and vegetal life unlike anything else in the world. But ignorance or insatiable curiosity have upset the fragile ecosystems of Bermuda, and much, having disappeared, is irretrievably lost.

When I took on the task of editing this book, I had no idea of just how much property the National Trust held, but I did realize how important it was to halt the voracious gobbling up of green space and the rapid deterioration of the island's delicate environment. The Bermuda of Wyeth and Winslow Homer no longer exists; that has been relegated to the archives and our collective memories. Today the simplicity of an earlier architecture which grew out of a response to climate and availability of building material, seems to be losing ground to architectural types that are not only insensitive to the landscape, but have no context in the frame of Bermuda's cultural history. There is an urgent need to protect what remains of historical buildings and an environment that cannot be recreated by man.

The purpose of this book is to impress upon all who read it, the urgency of the task that faces us. The book has been designed as a photographic journey through the houses, museums and properties of the Bermuda National Trust. For some it might be an introduction to Bermuda's unique architecture; for others perhaps an insight to the precarious balance between extinction or survival of the island's wetlands and nature preserves, since uncontrolled development driven by greed, has pushed this fragile ecosystem to the very edge. Above all, this book should serve to remind us of what we must protect and hold as sacred what must be *Held in Trust* for our progeny and for the generations yet to come.

Deborah St George Butterfield 1989

**Deborah died in 1995, but her words still ring true.
The first *Held in Trust* owed its existence to her drive
and persistence.**

Islands at the Edge, page 11. Foreword by Jacques Cousteau.
Published by Douglas & McIntyre, Vancouver/Toronto, 1984.

How it All Began

Recollections from the early days of the Trust

By WS Zuill, Sr, Director Emeritus

The community of Bermuda is held together by a network of mainly volunteer organisations which link individuals and groups. One of the largest and most respected of these is the Bermuda National Trust, whose particular endeavours are to preserve our natural and built heritage.

The story began more than 70 years ago, in 1937, when the conservation of our culture took a new and important turn with the formation of the Bermuda Historical Monuments Trust, which aimed to safeguard Bermuda's heritage through ownership of historically important houses and open spaces. It was an extremely successful venture, leading to the acquisition of a number of significant historic buildings, as well as major portions of Spittal Pond and Paget Marsh. The full story of the Monuments Trust is told on page 5. However in 1968, when Bermuda embraced its new constitution the decision was taken to create a new organisation to replace it. The Monuments Trust was able to pass on its properties and collections to this new membership organisation, the Bermuda National Trust.

The constitution of the National Trust, which is set out in an Act of Parliament, was based on the English Trust, which in turn was based on the constitution of the Trustees of Reservations of Massachusetts. In Bermuda's case the Trust is governed by a 13-person Council, consisting of three members appointed by the Government, five by the founding societies (Bermuda Audubon Society, Bermuda Garden Club, Bermuda Historical Society, Keep Bermuda Beautiful, and St George's Historical Society), and five elected by the membership at annual general meetings. The President is chosen by the Council.

The Bermuda National Trust Act 1969 gave the Trust extraordinary powers — most notably the power to declare property inalienable. Once the Trust Council has made this declaration about a property the Trust owns, it cannot be sold or mortgaged. In 1982 an amendment to the Trust Act was passed to give the Trust additional power to protect buildings and open space by entering into conservation agreements with landowners in which the subject property is protected by a covenant.

Among the responsibilities of the Monuments Trust were the national archives, but these, it was felt, should be in the hands of a government department rather than the newly formed Bermuda National Trust. The Monuments Trust, however, had acquired more than just the government archives; it had obtained a number of important paintings and documents from private collections. It was agreed that these would remain the property of the National Trust, but be kept in the Archives, an arrangement which continues to this day.

By 1970 the Monuments Trust had acquired 34 acres of land and seven important structures, with a number of minor ones. It had also been given the oversight of the military and naval cemeteries as British troops withdrew from the island. It was an impressive foundation for the new National Trust, which was about to develop in its own right. It started with a membership of 325, which rapidly increased in the first five years to 1,700. Acreage grew to 63, including the 9.6 acres of the Keep (site of today's Bermuda Maritime Museum) which Government leased to the Trust in 1974, an indication of its respect for the new organisation.

Today the Trust is responsible for a landholding of 240 acres of open space, 55 historic buildings, and an annual turnover of nearly $3 million — a testament to 70 years of work and careful stewardship, 37 years since the National Trust was formed. Some notable additions to the property portfolio have included Tivoli, Locust Hall and its farm, other parts of Devonshire Marsh and land surrounding Warwick Pond. Much of this success is due to the work of volunteers in many areas and the backing of good friends including Bermuda's corporate citizens, both local and international. In addition, the Trust has developed a professional staff to manage its business day to day.

Members are essential if the Trust's voice is to have meaning and credibility with the public and the Government. The Trust worked hard at developing membership, setting up membership tables at all likely events, providing frequent mailings, joining up cultural group visitors from overseas, and promoting life memberships, which in the early days were a bargain at $100 an individual.

Members were attracted when the Trust's voice started to be heard urging the preservation of open land and historic buildings, and the Department of Planning found backing for its work from the Trust, although by no means did the Trust always agree with the planners! People joined the Trust as a means of making their voices heard, and sometimes withdrew if they disagreed with the Trust.

Events were devised for members, such as the Spittal Pond nature walk for children during the winter half-term, and the Palm Sunday walk which introduced members to parts of Bermuda they could not normally reach. The Christmas Party in St George's, designed to entertain our more than 1,000 members with events in each of the major St George's properties, became very popular. The museums would be lit by candlelight and there would be live 18th century music. Refreshments, provided by volunteers, would be served. The idea caught on, and pretty soon St Peter's Church and the St George's Historical Society museum opened their doors and were lit by candlelight. Shops took advantage of the opportunity and started opening until the 'Trust Christmas Party' became the 'Christmas Walkabout'.

Fund raising was an important part of the Trust's work from the beginning, but it took some 18 years before the Trust really became successful at this. By then Bermuda was starting to enjoy the fruits of the international company business and more money became available for charities. At the same time large fund-raising events began to take place annually, giving the Trust an opportunity to make itself known among the offshore businesses.

An annual auction and sale during the winter was introduced by members who enjoyed attending auctions anyway. At first all items were donated; later it was agreed that a portion of the profits would go to donors who requested it. Tied in with the auction were a jumble sale and a plant and bake sale, the latter at a different venue and on a different day. All have proved successful, raising much-needed revenue.

Another aspect of fund raising which also kept the Trust's name before the public was the start of Trust shops. Trust items had been sold at the museums and at Waterville, but this was replaced by a far more professional — albeit carried out entirely by volunteers — approach. 'Trustworthy' shops were opened in Hamilton and later in St George's with interesting and different merchandise which attracted good custom.

With more money the Trust was able to improve its work in restoring old buildings and was also able to launch an education programme, including summer Trust weeks and other events for young people. This also attracted young archaeologists, for a growing band of members began digging around Trust properties and in basements, shedding light on such questions as how 18th century Bermudians fed themselves. (One answer was "mainly on fish" for fish bones mingled with rat bones in places where the archaeologists discovered rubbish dumps.)

Publications are part of the educational work, of which this volume is an example. *Held in Trust* was originally published to coincide with an International Conference of National Trusts staged in Bermuda, another sign of the Trust's success. Other books have been published, too, notably Bryden Hyde's *Bermuda's Antique Furniture and Silver*, *The Rich Papers*, 17th century correspondence, and, with the Bermuda Historical Society, a third edition of Governor Lefroy's *Memorials of the Bermudas*, a compilation of government documents. Another important addition to knowledge about Bermuda is the Trust's *Bermuda's Architectural Heritage* series of carefully researched books about the buildings in the different parishes which display Bermuda's native architecture.

You can see from all this what a widespread organisation the Trust has become. A staff member of the English National Trust once said: "Our organisational plans, with interlocking responsibilities, look as if they couldn't work. We only succeed because of enormous reservoirs of good will." When you think of the many volunteers working in different areas, and the many committees of our Trust you realise what an unwieldy organisation it could be — and so we, too, continue to work thanks to a broad reservoir of good will.

William Zuill was the first Director of the Bermuda National Trust, retiring in 1990.

The Bermuda Historical Monuments Trust

The Bermuda Historical Monuments Trust was founded in 1937 by Dr Henry Wilkinson with the support of the St George's and the Bermuda Historical Societies. He had been inspired by a visit to Colonial Williamsburg in Virginia where he had been conducting research. The Monuments Trust was created by an Act of Parliament but was designed to be independent of the Government. The seven trustees were appointed by the Governor. Like the Colonial Williamsburg Foundation, this was not an organisation which sought members; rather it relied on the help of the Bermuda Government and the purses of its board members to fund purchases. Whenever the Monuments Trust members contemplated a major project, they would brief the Finance Committee of the House of Assembly and funds would normally be forthcoming. It was a relationship to be envied.

The old town of St George's was its initial focus, primarily based on concern for the State House, one of the oldest standing stone structures erected by English colonists in the New World. The Trust managed to protect the ancient monument from incompatible development in the vicinity by acquiring buildings around it, but the fact that they did not control the building itself created decades of frustration. The Trust had commissioned a sketch plan for restoration of the State House in 1938, and 30 years later, as the Monuments Trust was about to be wound up, they were just closing in on getting the job done. The completion of the project was finally reported in the summer 1972 issue of the Bermuda National Trust newsletter.

Throughout the life of the Monuments Trust, its members were as concerned with preserving historical records as they were with buildings. They arranged for the consolidation of the Colonial Records, were instrumental in the building of a fireproof addition to the Bermuda Library, and engaged an archivist. Over the years many vital records were repaired and transcribed and are used today as basic research tools.

The first building acquired by the Monuments Trust was Tucker House in 1939. It was chosen for its connection to the Tucker family and the quality of the building itself. In 1947 local businessman and artist Hereward Watlington reached agreement with Robert Tucker, a descendant in possession of many family portraits, furniture and silver, that he would bequeath these Tucker artefacts to the Monuments Trust so that a museum could be established at Tucker House to display them. This was the beginning of the Trust's collections, and over the years many more paintings, maps, silver, furniture were added.

The 1950s was a decade of major acquisitions of historic buildings: the Old Rectory in 1950, and the Globe Hotel, Buckingham and Verdmont in 1951. The final two major acquisitions were Waterville in 1962 and Springfield in 1966. Hereward Watlington also wanted to preserve Palmetto House which he was able to lease, and he financed and oversaw work to protect the building. It finally came into the ownership of the Bermuda National Trust in 1970. Not content with preserving Bermuda's architecture and history, Dr Wilkinson was concerned about saving Bermuda's dwindling open space. He devoted years to the acquisition of Paget Marsh and bought the first segment of Spittal Pond, which was conveyed to the Trust in 1973.

The trustees of the Monuments Trust gave generously of their own time, money, skills and expertise to repair and furnish the properties and carry out all the other work of the Trust. Dr Wilkinson was the driving force, and he put a great deal of his own money into it. Hereward Watlington, WES Zuill, Sir Stanley Spurling, Dr Dunbar Bell, Leslie Darling, Wilfred Onions, and later, William S Zuill and David Wingate, all contributed, providing funding, time and skills.

When Bermuda embraced a new constitution in 1968 it became obvious that the Monuments Trust would fall under the control of a cabinet member and would cease to be an essentially autonomous semi-private organisation. The original idea for the formation of a national organisation to protect Bermuda's built and natural heritage came from the Conservation Committee of the Garden Club of Bermuda, and they were quickly joined by the Bermuda Audubon Society and the Bermuda Historical Society. Keep Bermuda Beautiful and the St George's Historical Society were soon invited to join. Planning started in 1967, the Act was passed in 1969 and in 1970 the Bermuda National Trust came into being. The rest, as they say, is history.

CHAPTER 1

HISTORIC PROPERTIES

T he Bermuda National Trust cares for an important collection of old Bermuda buildings, many in St George's but others throughout the island. Most of them date from the 18th century or even earlier and together they make up a unique portfolio. Some were acquired through the foresight of the Bermuda Historical Monuments Trust, some were purchased by the National Trust, often on favourable terms, and some were donated. Others, sometimes of less architectural

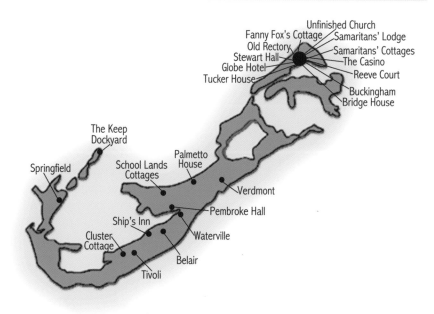

interest, have come to the Trust because they were on land being acquired as nature reserves or other open space. While a number of the properties have been let on long leases with protective covenants, most are maintained by the Trust. With a few welcome and notable exceptions, no other old buildings in Bermuda have had their integrity so carefully preserved. Modern windows and other innovations have proved too tempting for many owners of old buildings, and even the listing of buildings by the Bermuda Government has not preserved some of the best. So the Trust's buildings become even rarer as time passes.

Bermuda's architecture is unique and often said to be its only indigenous art. The skills of builders as familiar with ship building as with house building, the available materials of cedar and limestone with their limitations, the lack of formally trained architects, the likelihood of hurricanes, the island's isolation from the mother country of the first settlers all combined to create a truly original and distinctive vernacular architecture suited both to the humble cottage and the grander two-storey house.

Maintenance of such buildings is expensive, and sometimes the superficial upkeep lags, but over the years fund-raising campaigns have ensured that all the Trust's buildings are structurally sound and fitted for appropriate use in the 21st century. It is hoped that future fund-raising campaigns will build endowment funds for each building. The Trust believes that gentle maintenance and repair is important. Whenever possible old roofs and beams should be retained, being strengthened when necessary, old windows patched rather than replaced, and old floors and porches cherished. The over-implementation of modern engineering standards and the availability of non-traditional building supplies have contributed to the degradation of much of Bermuda's architectural heritage, and financial help from the Government to encourage the maintenance of listed buildings has been minimal.

The following pages provide a record of the Trust's buildings, showing both how wonderful they are in their own right, and how important they are to Bermuda as daily reminders of our rich man-made heritage. *Margaret Lloyd*

Buckingham

2 King Street, St George's
Grade 2 Listed Building

The Bermuda Historical Monuments Trust worked hard to protect the area around the State House (pictured opposite, bottom right), one of the oldest remaining stone structures built by English colonists in the New World. Built 1620-21, it had been much altered over the centuries but was still considered historically important. In the early 1970s the State House was reconstructed, using the illustration on John Smith's 1624 map as a guide. To preserve the building's rightful position and prevent incompatible development nearby, over time the Monuments Trust purchased several of the buildings surrounding the State House. Buckingham, acquired in 1951, stands in front of the State House making it key to this campaign. Completed around 1750, it remains much the same as when it was built.

When the site was granted by the Crown to Thomas Brooke, Collector of Customs, in 1703 it was vacant. When his widow sold it on to Samuel Mills in 1745, it must still have been vacant, as the sale price was just £5. It was Mills who built Buckingham, a rather plain two-storey Georgian house. The house and land later belonged to his wife, and then to their son, Samuel Jr, a mariner. He and his wife Sarah lived at Buckingham with their sons Samuel III and Thomas Burt.

By 1803 the house was owned by Thomas Burt Mills, the builder's grandson. Known as a huckster, he accrued large business debts and mortgaged Buckingham to his neighbours William and Henry Todd. They eventually seized and sold the property and it passed through several other owners until William Hayward Fox, a victualler, bought the property at auction in 1833 and operated his dry goods store out of the basement. Fox and his family lived upstairs, adding a kitchen wing to the north during the 1860s. In those days, according to an 1854 map, there was a building (or two) on what is now the garden in front of the house, so the whole area would have felt very different. Today a bust of Tom Moore sits at the centre of the attractively planted area. (See picture on page 14.)

Samuel Crofts Rankin bought the house in 1901 and named it Buckingham. The name may have been intended to complement another property he owned called Windsor. The upper floors were used as a boarding house and the house gradually became more and more run down. His estate had still not been settled 45 years after his death and eventually two of his heirs petitioned, resulting in a court-mandated auction at which the Historical Monuments Trust purchased the property.

The building was restored in 1996 and the lower floor improved in 2004 by the Masterworks Foundation, a Bermudian not-for-profit arts organisation. The upper floors are rented as a residence and business premises, while the basement is the apartment for Masterworks' Artist in Residence.

The Casino

Built around 1716, the Casino is a typical 18th century merchant's house situated conveniently close to the wharf-side, with living quarters above and storage area below. It is a good example of an early building which has survived relatively unchanged. It has a characteristic 18th century chimney at its western end with two simple lines of necking close together and a Flemish gable at its eastern end.

Captain Robert Burton was granted the land in 1713 on the condition that he build a house within three years. He did not live to see the building completed but he asked in his will for his widow Esther to finish the house, which she did. She then married a Thomas Smith and they lived at the Casino. Esther Smith left the house to her granddaughter, another Esther, Mrs George Ball. Esther and George mortgaged the house in 1768 to George Forbes, but all did not go smoothly and in 1781 they were sued for the money by Forbes' heirs. Their son Alexander Forbes Ball inherited the house, only to have to mortgage it soon after, and in 1824 the house was put up for sale.

The silversmith Joseph Gwynn was the purchaser. One evening, this pillar of the community became enraged when his son was sentenced to a gaol term by Magistrate Dr Joseph Hunter. Gwynn set off to confront Hunter but could not find him. On his way back to the Casino, Gwynn mistook his neighbour Henry Folger for Hunter and shot him dead at point blank range. Gwynn escaped the scene and hid for weeks. Eventually he was caught when his wife was observed passing food through a trapdoor to his hiding place in the cellar by an officer on a nearby hill watching the house with a telescope. The small community of St George's was rocked by this murder, the first of a Bermudian in 20 years. Gwynn was sentenced to be hanged at the site of the murder, the corner of Duke of York and Princess Streets. (See page 128.)

The Casino was forfeited to the Crown and sold at auction in 1826 to William Tucker who later inherited nearby Reeve Court. He sold it 23 years later to James Mitchell, a discharged soldier turned grocer, who lived there with his wife and six children. Mitchell's children moved away but victualler Thomas Foster wanted the building for a liquor shop, so he tracked them down and bought their shares in 1882. In 1920 Foster sold the property to Reginald Higinbothom who ran it as a hotel and tavern. That is when it acquired its name, attributed to the illegal gambling that took place on the premises.

The Historical Monuments Trust acquired the property in 1966 to help with the restoration of the State House (pictured top left). This was achieved by using part of the Casino as a replacement for the State House's ante-room, which was subsequently demolished, thereby returning the State House to its original architectural footprint. The National Trust leased the Casino to the Jehovah's Witnesses in 1980 on a long lease.

Bridge House

Bridge House was originally a timber framed two-storey house built by Roger Bailey, a planter and shoemaker. The exact date of its construction is not known, but it was certainly there by the time of Richard Norwood's 1662-63 survey.

Bailey died in 1686, leaving the house to his wife, then to his sons, and specified that it not be 'sould to any straunger'. His descendants did not seem to feel as strongly about the house, and in 1702 Captain John Ffollett and his wife Jane bought the property from Bailey's son Aaron. Ffollett, an English merchant, had been deported to Barbados for his involvement in the Monmouth Rebellion, an attempt to overthrow England's King James II. He had prospered there and in 1702 he and his wife moved to Bermuda. The Ffolletts embarked on major reconstruction of the house in stone, but it had not been completed by the time they both died. In Jane's will, dated 1705, she asked that her close friend and neighbour Elizabeth Holland of Reeve Court oversee the work. The refitting of the house was completed in 1708 and the property was considered grand enough to become the residence of Governor Bennett, who lived there, possibly until his death in 1736.

By 1742 the house had been sold and John Esten was living there. Esten was a prominent merchant whose career included terms as Mayor and on Bermuda's governing body of the day, the Governor's Council. He was also a Judge of the Court of Vice-Admiralty. In June 1776, when the royal sloop of war *Nautilus* brought in her first American prize to the Admiralty court he resigned his commission "by reason of his interests in the American trade". Esten didn't own the house; the owner was Robert Dinwiddie, a Scot who served as Collector of Customs in Bermuda, and eventually became Governor of Virginia. In 1748 Esten's heirs and Dinwiddie swapped Bridge House for a wharf which no longer exists, so it did eventually belong to the Esten family.

In 1782, John Esten Jr sold Bridge House to the American Loyalist Bridger Goodrich. After escaping from gaol in Baltimore, where he was imprisoned as a traitor, Goodrich had become a successful privateer preying on American shipping. He infuriated the influential Tucker family, most of whom were staunch supporters of the Revolutionary cause, as he first captured Bermuda ships and then married their cousin Elizabeth Tucker.

Bridge House, known at the time as Town House, was sold out of the Goodrich family in 1817 to silversmith George Rankin, one of whose spoons is in the Trust's collections. His shop was on the property. Rankin's daughter Henrietta lived on at Bridge House until she was 98 years old. On her death it was purchased by Frank Gurr, a St George's merchant. In 1968 he sold it to one of the founders of the Monuments Trust, Hereward Watlington, who sold it to the National Trust on very generous terms in 1971. Today's name for the house is thought to refer to a bridge which used to exist nearby.

Reeve Court

3 King Street, St George's
Grade 2 Listed Building

The early history of Reeve Court gives us a glimpse into the peripatetic lives of the early Bermuda merchants. The Reverend Thomas Holland built the house in 1705, and was granted the land on which it sat a year later. Despite this, the following year Holland and his wife Elizabeth left Bermuda for Virginia, selling the house to Samuel Smith of Pembroke who was a Colonel, Judge, Collector of Customs and member of the Governor's Council. For the next 50 or so years the house was owned by Smith's son, a merchant in Guadeloupe, and eventually his grandchildren.

Dr Richard Tucker of the Devonshire branch of the Tucker family had acquired the house by 1760, later taking his family to St Eustatius where he died in 1782. He left Reeve Court to his widow Mary, who returned to Bermuda that year. Their daughter Elizabeth also came back to Bermuda for long enough to marry the merchant Thomas Reeve, and then the couple left again, this time for St Croix where Reeve started a shipping business. It is thought Thomas and Elizabeth returned from St Croix around 1800 and she lived in the house until her death in 1844.

Elizabeth's much younger brother William Tucker, a successful merchant and at one time Justice of the Peace and a magistrate in St George's, inherited the house. He also owned the Casino and many other St George's properties. William's first wife, Hester Louisa Tucker, was known as Nea, and she is believed to be the Nea to whom the Irish poet Thomas Moore (left) wrote his *Odes to Nea*, containing such florid verses as "Behold the leafy mangrove, bending/O'er the waters blue and bright/Like Nea's silky lashes, lending/Shadow to her eyes of light!"

William's son, Territt Fraser Tucker, inherited Reeve Court and lived there with his wife Sofia. She occupied the house until her death. When her daughter Catherine married Frederick Basham in 1890, the Bashams bought out Catherine's brothers' and sisters' shares in the house.

The building is significantly larger than most buildings in St George's and was for centuries the tallest building in the town. There are two gardens, one for fruit and the other a parterre. The grounds seem small for such a large building, and it is thought that the lot to the rear of Reeve Court may once have been part of the property. The garden walls and old steps give great character to the house, and add to the architectural appeal of the town. The National Trust purchased Reeve Court in 1987, as part of the continuing strategy to protect the State House. An archaeological dig in 1990-91 revealed an 18th century livestock watering trough and a mid 17th century grave, as well as ceramics. The Trust carried out a complete restoration of the building in 1999, and it currently houses the laboratory of the Bermuda National Trust Archaeological Research Committee (see page 116) and two residential apartments.

President Henry Tucker House

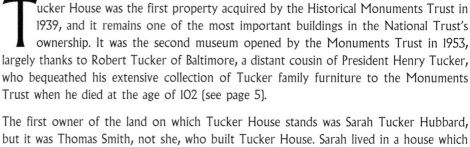

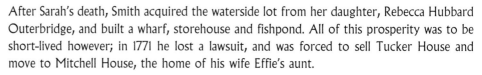

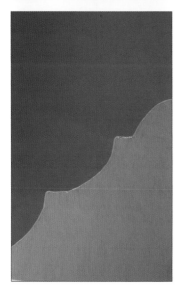

Tucker House was the first property acquired by the Historical Monuments Trust in 1939, and it remains one of the most important buildings in the National Trust's ownership. It was the second museum opened by the Monuments Trust in 1953, largely thanks to Robert Tucker of Baltimore, a distant cousin of President Henry Tucker, who bequeathed his extensive collection of Tucker family furniture to the Monuments Trust when he died at the age of 102 (see page 5).

The first owner of the land on which Tucker House stands was Sarah Tucker Hubbard, but it was Thomas Smith, not she, who built Tucker House. Sarah lived in a house which no longer exists on the waterside lot. In 1752 her daughters sold the northern part of the property to merchant and mariner Captain Thomas Smith, who built Tucker House largely as it exists today.

The building is a typical merchant's house with cellars below and living quarters above. It has a steeply pitched hip roof on the south side, with a double-flue chimney at the west end and lateral steps up to a simple porch, in a style which was common in St George's because of the constraints of the narrow streets. The Flemish gables at the rear of the house may have been inspired by the architecture of the Dutch colonies to which Smith's merchant career took him, but they could just have been copied from the Globe Hotel.

After Sarah's death, Smith acquired the waterside lot from her daughter, Rebecca Hubbard Outerbridge, and built a wharf, storehouse and fishpond. All of this prosperity was to be short-lived however; in 1771 he lost a lawsuit, and was forced to sell Tucker House and move to Mitchell House, the home of his wife Effie's aunt.

The Collector of Customs, Thomas Smith of Verdmont, owned Tucker House for a short time, but sold it in 1775 to Henry Tucker and his wife Frances, the daughter of Governor Bruere. In 1770 this well-connected man had been appointed Colonial Treasurer by his father-in-law, becoming a member of the Governor's Council the following year. Thanks to the influence of his own father, he also held the posts of Secretary and Provost Marshal, which came with a handsome salary. In the 1790s he was appointed President of the Council and, occasionally, Acting Governor.

Almost immediately after Henry moved in to Tucker House, the notorious Gunpowder Plot blew up. During the American Revolution, Bermuda was fearful of losing trade with the American colonies on which they depended for food as well as profit. Colonel Henry Tucker, President Henry's father, led a delegation to Philadelphia to plead Bermuda's cause. The Americans needed munitions, and soon afterwards a group of Bermudians stole gunpowder from the arsenal above Tobacco Bay and sent it to the Revolutionary American forces in Boston. It was an embarrassing state of affairs for the son-in-law of the

British Governor, but in the tense times that followed, President Henry is believed to have helped calm the situation in spite of the widespread belief that his brother St George was somehow involved.

As their family grew Henry and Frances needed to expand Tucker House. They added outbuildings, and a long extension to the north on the western side, only half of which survives. At the same time, the living quarters were upgraded. In 1807, having decided to move to England, Henry put Tucker House up for lease, but he died unexpectedly of influenza in February 1808. In 1809 his widow Frances sold the house to an agent of Gosling & Co, but when the firm went bankrupt and he could not pay the mortgage, she was forced to foreclose. In 1813 the house was sold again, this time to Liverpool merchant James Richardson. In 1825 Benjamin Dickinson Harvey, ship owner and lawyer, bought the house. He lived in Hamilton Parish but some of his 11 children lived at Tucker House. In his work as a lawyer, he was described as a champion of American causes in the Bermudian courts, and came under criticism for being 'a most determined Democrat'. He served as a Member of the House of Assembly for some 40 years. After his sudden death in 1833, his daughter Althea lived in the house.

In 1860 Tucker House was briefly sold to brothers William Tudor Tucker and the Reverend Richard Tucker, sons of the William Tucker who had earlier owned both the Casino and Reeve Court. They sold the house back to Althea but kept the waterside lot and the land to the north fronting on York Street. When Althea died in 1876, her nephew Captain Aubrey Harvey Tucker of the 68th Regiment of Foot sold the house to an Irishman from Londonderry, Robert Boggs, keeper of the new prison which had been built at the foot of Rose Hill. It was the daughter of Robert Boggs who sold the house to the Historical Monuments Trust in 1953, although she lived out her life there.

During Althea's tenure, Tucker House housed another notable person: Joseph Hayne Rainey was a free black man who left his native South Carolina during the American Civil War to avoid forced labour on seaport fortifications. In Bermuda he worked as a barber, renting the detached kitchen at Tucker House as a barber shop, while his wife built her reputation as a skilled dressmaker. Rainey was self-educated, and drew on the knowledge of the merchants of the town to further his education. After the Civil War, the Raineys returned to the US where he became the first black member of the House of Representatives. A bust of Rainey (left) is on display in the kitchen.

Tucker House has two small gardens enclosed within characteristic St George's courtyard walls and planted with herbs and perennials found in Bermuda in the 18th century. The house is furnished with furniture, paintings and silver which belonged to the Tucker family, collected by President Henry's sister, Frances. There are portraits by Joseph Blackburn of members of the Tucker family. Some of the china bears the Tucker family crest, and there are two handsome chandeliers, one of which is made of Waterford glass. The most recent addition to the collection is a fine portrait of Governor Bruere, donated by David L White, a past President of the Bermuda National Trust.

The Trust's Archaeological Research Committee have carried out archaeological digs at Tucker House and the basement of the building houses an interesting display of the results (see left and page 130).

Pearlware Handpainted Punch Bowls
Chinese Motif
English

Stewart Hall

5 Queen Street, St George's
Grade 1 Listed Building

Stewart Hall is one of the largest and most elegant early 18th century houses in St George's, and it was home to some prominent men. It is not known when the house was built, but it was already standing when the land was granted to Walter Mitchell in 1707 "in consideration of the great charges in erecting a substantiall building near the town church". The building has two storeys, with a gable roof and large chimneys at either end. The staircase and intricate cedar work on the interior are of particular interest. This was Walter Mitchell's first house, but he went on to build the new Government House and Mitchell House, now a museum operated by the St George's Historical Society.

Walter Mitchell was a third generation Bermudian, his grandfather having been one of the first colonists who came out on the ship the *Plough* in 1612. He married a wealthy widow, the daughter of a very early Sheriff, John Hubbard, who held the post of Taster and Tryer of Tobacco for Hamilton Parish. Mitchell prospered in business and died in 1731, one of the richest men in Bermuda. His will listed 36 chairs and four round tables on the ground floor of Stewart Hall, which would have left little space for anything else. The outbuilding is thought to have housed Mitchell's slaves. His widow left the house to her daughter who sold it to George Tucker in 1751 when she emigrated to the US with her husband.

George Tucker was the Colonial Secretary, Provost Marshal and a member of the Governor's Council. He lived at Stewart Hall with his wife, five children and 11 slaves. He made many changes to the interior configuration of the house, bringing it up to date in the Georgian style, and kept cattle in the courtyard. He died in 1766 and his widow lived on at the house for another 21 years.

The next prominent resident was Captain Andrew Durnford of the Royal Engineers, who was in Bermuda to rebuild the island's forts. He lived at Stewart Hall with his mistress Elizabeth Lucas and at least four children, despite the fact that he had a wife and children back in England. When he moved to his own house in 1793, Stewart Hall went up for auction and was bought by a niece of George Tucker. Over the next century it passed through the hands of a purser in the Royal Navy, a silversmith and a barrister. The barrister was Duncan Stewart, and although he never lived in the house, he gave it his name. The house underwent improvements and additions over the years, and ended up with seven chimneys in total.

The Historical Monuments Trust purchased Stewart Hall in 1949. It has undergone some major rehabilitation thanks to the National Trust's *In Trust for All* fund-raising campaign in the early 1990s. For many years the building housed the St George's branch of the Bermuda Library. Today the tenant is the Bermuda Perfumery, a relationship which has resulted in extensive improvements to the building and its gardens.

Samaritans' Lodge

29 Water Street, St George's
Grade 1 Listed Building

After emancipation, benevolent societies were lifelines to black Bermudians. They were linked with Friendly Societies in England and the US, mutual self-help groups which acted as informal insurance providers. One of the most important in Bermuda was the Independent Order of Good Samaritans (IOGS), together with its sister organisation, the Daughters of Samaria (DS). There were at least eight chapters of the Order in Bermuda. In St George's, the Samaritans' chapter was Rechab Lodge 7, founded in 1876, with its sister chapter, Princess Louise Lodge 12. The Order provided vital services such as medical care, education and help with funeral expenses.

Samaritans' Lodge itself started out as a storehouse built by John Davenport around 1844. It was sold at auction in 1900, and bought by the Samaritans. It took a few years to remove the tenants, who were using it as a workshop, and to renovate the building. The Samaritans added the fanlight and sidelights which give the front of the building such character, and they took occupancy in 1907. 'IOGS & DS' is still proudly displayed over the door.

The building is a good example of a late 19th century lodge building, and is today substantially as it was when it was in use by the Samaritans. It is L-shaped, with a hipped roof, the typical St George's eaves, pilasters and heavy hood moulds over the windows.

When the Trust bought the Lodge in 1977, it was somewhat dilapidated. After extensive renovations, the Trust used the building as a workshop once again. However, it was destined for a higher purpose, and when the Bermudian Heritage Museum was founded in 1994, it was clear that Samaritans' Lodge was the ideal site for a museum dedicated to the history of the Friendly Societies and to the heritage and accomplishments of black Bermudians.

Samaritans' Cottages

27 Water Street, St George's
Grade 1 Listed Building

The Samaritans' Cottages are fine examples of early 18th century cottages in the prevailing architectural style of St George's when the town was rebuilt in stone.

The eastern cottage dates back at least to 1704, and possibly to 1676 when William Pearman purchased a building on this site. The western cottage was built by Pearman's daughter Martha and her husband Thomas Handy in 1719. The lot on which it stood had belonged to an accused witch with the highly topical name of Potter. In 1693 Margery Potter was cleared of the charge of casting spells on one John Middleton and she lived on, passing the land to her daughter who in turn gave part of it to her niece, Martha Handy.

The two cottages remained under separate ownership until 1786, when Benjamin Fox acquired both properties, and they were sold together in 1806 to John Trott. In 1820 John Davenport acquired them, adding them to other properties he owned in the vicinity, including the storehouse which was to become Samaritans' Lodge. He probably rented them out as four or more units. When the Samaritans bought the Lodge in 1900, they also bought the eastern cottage. During the 20th century both the cottages and the Lodge fell into ruinous condition and were threatened with demolition. In order to save these important historic buildings, the National Trust bought them, making the two cottages one unit and letting it on a long lease to fund restoration of the property.

Davenport Cottage (pictured immediate right) shares a wall with the Samaritans' Cottages. It was built in the 1930s and was left to the National Trust by Dr Raymond Spurling. While not being of particular historic note in itself, its preservation is important in order to protect the historic fabric of this ancient part of St George's.

The Globe Hotel

32 York Street, St George's
Grade 1 Listed Building

T he Globe Hotel has a long and colourful history. Built in 1699 by Governor Samuel Day, it now houses the Bermuda National Trust Museum and Trustworthy shop. It is notable as one of the few large, early, stone buildings in which a double span of cedar was used to make a gable roof that covered two rooms. It is also thought to show the first use of Flemish gables in Bermuda. The Globe stands today much as it was built. As Dr Michael Jarvis says in *Bermuda's Architectural Heritage: St George's*: "Although he left much to be desired as a governor, Samuel Day as architect produced a finely proportioned residence which contrasted sharply with traditional Bermudian methods."

When Day was appointed Governor in 1697, the first Government House, built in 1612, was uninhabitable, and so he set about building a new one. The house was located on Crown land, built by the King's slaves — whose labour was a privilege of the Governor's office — with materials taken from Crown lands and the King's quarries. In spite of this, Day refused to vacate the building when he was replaced by Benjamin Bennett as Governor. To the dismay of his successor, Day's influential father convinced the Board of Trade in London to grant him ownership of the house. In the course of the dispute, however, Day was arrested for debt and imprisoned on Castle Island where he died in 1703. His brother sold the building to the Tucker family, who owned it throughout the 19th century although after 1860 none of them lived there.

Despite Britain's neutrality in the American Civil War (1861-65), Bermudians tended to favour the South, and *The Royal Gazette* acclaimed Confederate victories and decried Yankee 'atrocities'. The upper floor of the Globe Hotel was used by Confederate Commercial Agent John Tory Bourne and Confederate Shipping Agent Major Norman Walker. From here they coordinated the shipment of munitions, clothing and other much-needed cargo through the blockade that the northern states' Union had established to starve the southern states' Confederacy. It was a turbulent yet profitable period in St George's history and the Globe was at the heart of it.

In 1867 the house was rented to Ralph Foster who opened it for business as the Globe Hotel. Various proprietors followed until 1899, when watchmaker Samuel Crofts Rankin bought the building from Dr William Henry Tucker, and Rankin's grandsons continued to operate the hotel.

The Historical Monuments Trust purchased the Globe in 1951 from Rankin's estate and ran it as the Confederate Museum. In 1996, the Bermuda National Trust carried out a total rehabilitation of the building and installed a new exhibit which tells the story of the blockade-running years from a Bermudian perspective: *Rogues and Runners: Bermuda and the American Civil War*.

The Old Rectory

1 Broad Alley, St George's
Grade 1 Listed Building

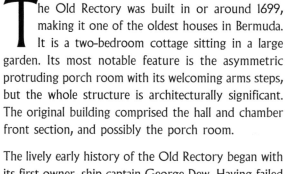

T he Old Rectory was built in or around 1699, making it one of the oldest houses in Bermuda. It is a two-bedroom cottage sitting in a large garden. Its most notable feature is the asymmetric protruding porch room with its welcoming arms steps, but the whole structure is architecturally significant. The original building comprised the hall and chamber front section, and possibly the porch room.

The lively early history of the Old Rectory began with its first owner, ship captain George Dew. Having failed as a privateer and slave trader, he came to Bermuda where he married, became a politician and fathered three children. The land was granted to him "in consideration of the great costs and sums laid out in buying one house" already on the site. In 1702 he left the house to his wife Ann.

From Dew's death, the records go silent until 1763, when the then-owner, mariner Richard Somersall, gave it to his daughter Ann and her husband, the Reverend Alexander Richardson, Rector of St George's. He initiated a major refurbishment of St Peter's Church and was known as the Little Bishop. It is his tenure that gave the cottage the name it has kept for two centuries, although it was never owned by the church and was never officially a rectory.

The Old Rectory has had two major refurbishments in its long history: one in the early 19th century and a second in the 1950s after it was bought by the Historical Monuments Trust. The land on which it sits has changed over the years as well. In the 1860s a portion of its garden was annexed to neighbouring Poinciana House and in 1903 land belonging to Whitehall was added to the Old Rectory. The current kitchen sits on the former Whitehall land. The garden is maintained as a traditional English cottage garden, the perfect setting for this charming cottage.

Fanny Fox's Cottage

10 Governor's Alley, St George's
Grade 1 Listed Building

This interesting cottage is an 18th century single storey house with an original kitchen behind the hall. It is a good example of how even small Bermudian houses tended to grow over time. The earliest part of the building, a two-room gable roof structure facing the road, dates from the early 18th century but there were additions up until the late 19th century. At the rear of the house it is possible to see the muddle of additions working together.

The lot of land was originally granted in 1700 to Provost Marshal Edward Jones, who was subsequently dismissed for gross negligence by Governor Benjamin Bennett. Jones was in charge of the gaol, but allowed the prisoners to come and go at will while he operated a dry goods store out of one of the cells. In 1706, after his dismissal, the lot was sold to James Burchall, a mariner. He built the core of the house – the north/south structure on the western side fronting the road. He left the house to his wife Martha and then to his son Elisha and other children.

By 1802 the house belonged to Henry Adams, master mariner. Adams' widow Sophia left the house to her husband's nephew Benjamin Fox when he came of age. He married Frances Zuill, known as Fanny, for whom the cottage is named. Legend has it that the marriage lasted only one night, and her comment on the situation was that "he was a no-good creature anyway". Whatever the case, Fanny lived in the house and inherited it on Benjamin's death. In 1835 she gave the cottage to her brother William Zuill, but she remained there until her old age when she moved back to her ancestral home, Orange Grove in Smith's Parish.

The cottage was purchased by the Historical Monuments Trust in May 1951. It was in poor repair at the time, and the Trust carried out an extensive renovation.

The Unfinished Church

1 Church Folly Lane, St George's
Listed as an Historical Monument

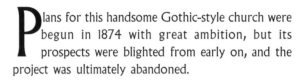

Plans for this handsome Gothic-style church were begun in 1874 with great ambition, but its prospects were blighted from early on, and the project was ultimately abandoned.

By the mid 19th century St Peter's Church had fallen into disrepair, and its congregation agreed to replace it. The new church was designed by architect William Hay of Edinburgh. It was to be a grand Gothic structure in cruciform style with a commanding tower, built on the site of the 1721 Government House.

Construction was already under way when a split in the congregation led to one faction forming the Reformed Episcopal Church, and building their own house of worship, now the Salvation Army Hall. In 1884 Trinity Church in Hamilton was destroyed by fire, and funds intended for the new St George's church were diverted to rebuild it. Despite these significant setbacks, the church was almost finished by 1894 and the roof went on in 1899, paid for by private donations. After all this, the project was still abandoned. The congregation decided that the original St Peter's would suit the community's needs perfectly well, and they turned their energies to renovating it, leaving the Unfinished Church to fall into ruin. Today, its location is the appropriately named Church Folly Lane.

The abandoned church was badly damaged in 1926 by a hurricane, but a photograph from 1953 shows the structure with its roof still largely intact. Since then the roof disappeared, the stonework weathered and the structure became a ruin. In 1990 Thalia (Tilly) Jones and her family and the Bermuda National Trust combined forces to save the structure, which was facing demolition. The Trust leased the property from the Anglican Church for 50 years and with funds provided by the Jones family carried out a restoration project to stabilise the structure, completing this work in 1997.

Verdmont

Collector's Hill, Smith's Parish
Grade 1 Listed Building

Verdmont is a grand mansion house built in the Georgian style by John and Elizabeth Dickinson some time between their marriage in 1693 and his death in 1714. It stood on 93 acres of land – stretching from the South Shore to Flatts – which had been previously owned by William Sayle. A prominent figure in the early days of the British colonies, he was Governor of South Carolina, and of Bermuda on three separate occasions.

To add an exotic element to the story, the funds used by the Dickinsons to buy the property resulted from a profitable piratical venture involving Bermudian ship, the *Amity*, in the Indian Ocean in 1691. Elizabeth's first husband and her father had both been shareholders in the *Amity*, and she was left a wealthy widow. Her second husband, Dickinson, was a ship owner and served as Speaker of the House of Assembly. At a time when most houses were small and located in protected areas, the Dickinsons built a grand house on top of a hill, with sweeping views over the South Shore. The Dickinsons lived at Verdmont with their two daughters, his unmarried sister, her slave Bess and six other slaves. John died in 1714, leaving the house for life to his wife. On her death one daughter, Elizabeth, was to inherit the house and 50 acres to the south. The other daughter, Mary, had the northern portion of the estate. At Verdmont, the mother Elizabeth lived with her daughter Elizabeth, son-in-law Perient Spofferth, their son and their daughter, also named Elizabeth. Elizabeth Dickinson outlived her daughter, and her granddaughter inherited Verdmont.

The heiress Elizabeth married Collector of Customs Thomas Smith in 1755, and they lived at Verdmont with the four daughters of his previous marriage. Smith's duties were carried out in Bermuda's only port of entry, St George's, and he owned Tucker House in the old

town for some years. The Smiths, along with their artistic son-in-law John Green, did a great deal to modernise Verdmont, bringing it to the fashionable standard of their time. The size of the establishment at Verdmont grew, and at Smith's death there were 14 slaves in the household.

The next notable Verdmont owner, John Green, came into the family when he married Smith's daughter Mary, who was known as Polly. Green, an Irishman, was a portrait painter who had artistic connections with the founders of the Royal Academy in London. After marrying, Polly and he lived at Verdmont with his in-laws and he painted the portraits of Smith and his daughters which hang in the house today. He briefly held the post of Collector of Customs, and then was made a Judge of the Vice-Admiralty Court. Green was deeply unpopular with American merchants, as they felt he always found for Bermudians and against Americans in cases involving prizes and privateering.

On the death of her stepmother in 1789, Polly inherited Verdmont and the portion of land north of the South Shore Road, and her cousin Samuel Henry Trott (son of one of Polly's sisters) got the land south of the road. The Greens both died within the next 14 years, and Trott moved into Verdmont, which he inherited in 1803, reuniting the two parts of the estate. Trott was a prominent man in his own right, serving as a magistrate and a member of the Colonial Parliament. He married Sarah Musson and they had many children, five of whom survived to adulthood. Trott was not a healthy man and he died in 1817, leaving his widow to live on at Verdmont. Her son John took over the estate when he married Harriet Brownlow in 1831, but theirs was not a happy life and in 1860, after the death of their second child, Verdmont was sold for the first time in its history.

The buyer was a farmer, Rupert Hugh Spencer, who lived at Verdmont with his widowed elder brother and his brother's two daughters, who would inherit the estate in 1868. Once again the estate was broken into two parts, divided by South Road, but this time it was forever. Emma Spencer had the northern portion with the house, and lived there with her husband Stafford Joell. They had five children, and left Verdmont to their two unmarried daughters, Lillian and Irene, in 1919. Lillian lived in Verdmont without electricity or running water for some 45 years. Every day she walked in to Hamilton to work as a secretary at a law firm. When it came time for her to move to Westmeath Nursing Home, she sold the property to her nephew, Alan Paul Joell. He sold the house and 2.3 acres to the Bermuda Historical Monuments Trust, subdividing the rest of the property into building lots.

The Monuments Trust bought this exceptional property both to preserve it and provide access for the public by turning it into a museum. The Monuments Trust formed a committee of their chairman Dr Henry Wilkinson, noted architect Wilfred Onions, and artist Hereward Watlington to manage the restoration. Repairs were carried out and a small balcony was added to the south side. Once the appropriate furnishings and John Green portraits had been acquired and the gardens landscaped, Verdmont was opened in 1957 as a museum, which it has been ever since. The old kitchen, which is thought to have been slave quarters, is now a part of the African Diaspora Heritage Trail, a transnational cultural tourism initiative.

Verdmont is correctly described as the jewel in the crown of the Bermuda National Trust, its most important building in a group of historically and architecturally significant buildings.

Palmetto House

74 North Shore Road, Devonshire
Grade 1 Listed Building

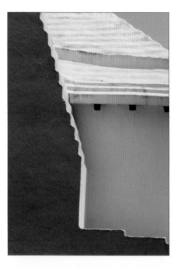

This handsome stone house was built around 1700 or soon after by a William Williams, the third or fourth of that name to own the land on which it stands. It is roughly cross-shaped in plan, and has long been regarded as one of the important early Bermuda cruciform buildings although it has hipped roofs rather than the more usual gable. There is also some question about whether the north wing was built at the same time as the rest of the house; if it was an addition, it was very early. In any case, it is a beautiful building which survives largely in its original condition, an outstanding example of early Bermudian architecture. The welcoming arms steps and mounting block below, the double-flue chimneys with simply finished necking and the windows tucked in under the eaves are all typical early 18th century features.

The last member of the Williams family to own the house was Benjamin S Williams. He was a prominent member of the community, serving as overseer of the roads, as well as church warden, choirmaster and organist at Devonshire Church. He married two ladies from the Cox family, the second of whom, Frances Cox Williams, is said to have married him to get even with him for mistreating his first wife, a relative and dear friend of hers. This seems almost plausible, given how eccentric Frances reportedly was, famously keeping her coffin underneath her bed and occasionally sleeping in it.

Palmetto House was one of the many buildings in Devonshire appropriated by the War Department for inclusion in the Prospect Garrison. Devonshire was the hardest hit of any parish by this programme; many families were evicted and in the end it turned out that some evictions may not even have been necessary. In 1868 Palmetto House was compulsorily purchased from the estate of Benjamin Williams, although it was further from Prospect than any other house seized. It was first used as the single officers' quarters, later becoming the club house for the Garrison Golf Course. In 1948, concerned about the run-down state of the house, Hereward Watlington came to the rescue. He rented the property and proceeded to reinstate the house to its former glory by undoing the alterations made by the military, and using appropriate replacement fittings and material from other sites to restore it. Ownership remained with the Crown Lands Corporation and then the Bermuda Government until it was purchased by the newly-formed Bermuda National Trust in 1970.

For many years it was the home of Wing Commander AM (Mo) Ware and his wife Sylvia. The senior RAF officer in Bermuda during the Second World War, Mo Ware was seconded to the Bermuda Government to oversee the conversion of the military airfield into a public airport. He remained in Bermuda after leaving the RAF, becoming Director of Civil Aviation for many years. Until very recently parts of his old aircraft could be found on the grounds of Palmetto House. At the time of the publication of this book the Trust is carrying out a major restoration of the house.

School Lands Cottages

2, 4, 6 School Lands Lane, Pembroke
Grade 2 Listed Buildings

These three small houses feature beautiful chimneys, an elegant buttery and an unusual set of lateral entrance steps of a style normally found only in St George's. The cottages were in poor condition in 1981 when the National Trust bought them for their historical and architectural significance. It has recently emerged that it was in the largest of these houses that the slave Mary Prince endured cruel treatment at the hands of 'Captain I' and his wife, as recounted in her famous narrative of 1831, *The History of Mary Prince, a West Indian Slave*. The fact that the connection was made with the building is testament to the formidable skills of the Trust's researchers for the *Bermuda's Architectural Heritage* book series.

When the Trust first became interested in the cottages, it was believed they had been built to generate income for the education of poor children. The land was thought to have been the 'ffree-schoole land' formerly belonging to Nicholas Ferrar, a religious man and a philanthropist. We now know that this is not so. In the course of plotting the shares of Richard Norwood's 1663 survey in Pembroke for the *Architectural Heritage* series, Trust researchers discovered that the School Lands shares were 19 and 20, while the cottages are all situated on share 21.

A portion of share 21 was owned by John Ingham. The 1789 assessment lists him as Mr John Ingham, but his second wife's obituary describes her as the widow of Captain Ingham. John Ingham owned the property until 1827 and lived there with his first wife Mary Spencer Albouy. Mary Prince's description leaves little doubt that this was the house in which she spent some miserable years. In Prince's *History*, she describes how after she was sold to a new owner in 1800, she was "given into the charge of his son, a lad about my own age, Master Benjy, who took me to my new home". Ingham's oldest child was Benjamin, who was baptised in 1790, and Mary Prince was born in about 1788. 'Captain I' and his wife were the worst kind of slave owners, gratuitously cruel to a willing young girl. Still, Mary Prince had worse to come: she was sold to a new owner who sent her to make salt in the Turks Islands, where she endured horrific hardship. In 1818, back in Bermuda, she was sold again. This owner eventually took her to London where she found shelter in a Moravian church and the opportunity to tell her story. Her *History* became the first published account of the life of a female slave, making a huge impact on the abolition movement and helping to create momentum for the emancipation of slaves. Slavery was finally abolished in the British Empire in 1834.

After the death of his first wife, John Ingham married again and had four more children. When he died in 1827 the property passed to his second son. It was later purchased by a Front Street merchant, and in the mid 20th century by Dr Edgar Campbell Wilkinson, remaining in the Wilkinson family until 1976. It is now on a long lease and under renovation.

Pembroke Hall

42 Crow Lane, Pembroke
Grade 2 Listed Building

Pembroke Hall is an elegant building set in manicured gardens at the entrance to Hamilton. The original U-shaped house was built in the late 18th or early 19th century. The house is set on a hill and the single-storey wing on the north side, with its old hipped roofs and pilasters, is the least altered part of the building today.

Cornelius Hinson owned the land all the way over to the North Shore at the time of his death in 1789 but it is likely that the present house was built by the next owner, Richard Wood, for his daughter Frances Russell Wood and her husband Joseph Dill. The Dills' daughter Frances and her husband Thomas Reid inherited it. Mrs Reid's brother, Lucius Dill, was a merchant in the West Indies and brought back many of the exotic trees which grace the grounds to this day.

When Frances Reid died in 1913 she left the house to her cousin Lieutenant Colonel Tom Dill, but the bulk of her fortune went to the Bermuda Cathedral endowment. For some of this period, the house was operated as a guest house. When Colonel Dill died in 1945, the property was left to his daughters.

In 1981 Fidelity International bought the house, giving the freehold to the Trust, and retaining a long lease on the property. Fidelity undertook a careful restoration and expansion of the house for use as their international headquarters. They restored the original façade, preserving the hipped roof and pilasters, meticulously restoring the woodwork in the reception rooms and adding a sympathetic extension at the rear. The old fishpond on the site has been preserved, and recently the boat house was rehabilitated.

This was a partnership model that has worked well for both parties, preserving a wonderful piece of Bermuda's architectural heritage for future generations.

Waterville and Waterville Park

2 Pomander Road, Paget
Grade 1 Listed Building

Headquarters of the Bermuda National Trust, and one of its finest properties, Waterville is among the oldest houses in Bermuda. The grounds, which are open to the public, include sweeping lawns, a rose garden, memorial benches and a gazebo. The house's wooden verandah with lattice porch and curved steps are among Waterville's most notable features.

Waterville is a Trimingham house, one of several grand houses owned by that prominent family in Paget. Seven generations of Triminghams had lived in Waterville before it was acquired by the Historical Monuments Trust in 1962. The family, starting with John Trimingham who arrived in Bermuda around 1620, acquired land in the Paget area, and eventually their property spanned the width of the island, from the South Shore to Hamilton Harbour. The land on which Waterville stands was acquired in the early 18th century.

John Trimingham, President of the Governor's Council in the late 1720s, built Waterville around 1720. He had held a privateer's commission from Queen Anne and had a profitable career at sea. His wealth enabled him to set up a successful shipping business. It is thought that he built Waterville for his daughter Jane at the time of her marriage to Conrad Jones. It was one of five houses he owned by his death in 1734, and in his will he bequeathed to his son John Jr "three shares and house wherein my daughter Jane Jones now dwells". The original house was L-shaped, comprising what is now the main and western wings. The Council met under a tamarind tree in the garden at Waterville while he was President.

John Jr was a judge in both the civil court and the Court of Vice-Admiralty. His son, another John Trimingham, was a sea captain who lived in the house until his death in 1798. He and his brothers continued the family's shipping activities and, although he died quite young, he succeeded in consolidating the family's wealth. Waterville is located on an inlet of Hamilton Harbour. The harbour was known as Crow Lane and Waterville's inlet was called simply The Lane. The family ships were built and docked there. The house was used like so many merchants' houses in that time: the lower floor for cargo storage with the family living in the quarters above.

John Jr's grandson, James Harvey Trimingham, lived at Waterville with his wife Charlotte, three sons, five daughters, and his mother Mary. Perhaps not surprisingly, he found it necessary to enlarge the house, and in 1811 he added an eastern wing and the unusual entrance porch, making Waterville U-shaped. He also upgraded the level of decoration of the moulding, doors and windows in the drawing room. On his death in 1829, the house passed to two of his sons, ultimately belonging to the next James Harvey Trimingham, who founded the famous Triminghams' retail establishment. His first shop opened in 1842 at Waterville, where everything 'from boots to bonnets' was sold. He lived at Waterville

with his first wife, Emily Hinson Gosling, who died in childbirth in 1845. He then married Helen Malvina Darrell and she raised his growing family, which eventually totalled 11 children. The store was moved to Hamilton to free space in the now rather crowded family home. On his death in 1899 he left a life interest in Waterville to his wife and three unmarried daughters Louisa, Charlotte and Helen. Louisa lived to the age of 96, and on her death in 1956 the house went to the surviving sons Brownlow and Reginald, and grandsons Harold, Kenneth and James.

Waterville became an exclusive guest house in the 1920s, with room to accommodate 13 guests. It was run by Frederick Brownlow Trimingham's American wife, Ada. The storage cellars were converted into the public rooms, with the bedrooms upstairs. Regular guests included the American cartoonist James Thurber and writer EB White. Hudson Strode, author of *The Story of Bermuda*, wrote of his stay at Waterville in 1946 and mentions the sisters Martha and Georgina who had worked at Waterville as cook and waitress for more than two decades. He said of Martha: "I learned immediately that she was a woman to be valued above rubies." Ada ran the guest house until her death in 1961.

After Ada's death, Waterville was purchased by the Historical Monuments Trust. This was made possible by the generosity of Kenneth, Eldon and Andrew Trimingham, who gave up their shares of the purchase price in order to make it possible to save this classic Bermudian building from alteration or demolition. Alice Emily Gosling (Elsie), granddaughter of Joseph L Trimingham, lived upstairs at Waterville until her death in 1990 at the age of 93, while the lower floor became the headquarters of the Bermuda National Trust.

Waterville is set in extensive gardens and Waterville Park includes Duck Island. The Park is a tribute to the continuing generosity of the Trimingham family; it was donated by deForest and Fenton Trimingham in 1983. The Rose Society's Repository Rose Garden, which is maintained by the Society, is west of the house. The eastern gardens and the gazebo comprise the Mary Jean Mitchell Green Memorial Garden, thanks to a generous gift from her family.

Belair

11 Cobbs Hill Road, Paget
Grade 2 Listed Building

Belair, on more than two acres on Cobbs Hill overlooking Hamilton Harbour, is a unique example in Bermuda of a West Indian plantation house. Surrounded by wide balconies, with a shallow sloping roof and extensive cellars, quoining on the corners and around the doors and surrounded by formal gardens, it is essentially unaltered today.

The builder Francis Albouy was a successful businessman in Demerara, but eventually returned to Bermuda where he served as a member of the Governor's Council for many years. Dr Henry Wilkinson says of him that he was given the chair at the 1844 inaugural meeting at Walsingham of the Royal Bermuda Yacht Club and comments "he had raced boats on the high seas during the Napoleonic wars when racing was for higher stakes than a silver cup". Albouy purchased nine acres of land in several pieces, on one of which was the building now known as Fourways, and he built Belair around 1815.

He died aged 80, leaving the property to his wife Ann for life, and then to his "kinsman and former partner in trade", Samuel Augustus Harvey, who inherited when Ann died in 1859. Harvey died in 1882 but his stepmother continued to live in the house for many years, so the house could not be sold by the estate.

Belair eventually came to be owned by an American, Lydia Moncure Robinson, who had inherited it from her father and used it as her winter residence. Thanks to a clause in Miss Robinson's will, the National Trust was allowed to purchase the building from her estate for less than its market value. It was still a formidable amount of money however, and the only way the Trust could manage the finances at the time was to sell a long lease on the property. This arrangement enabled the Trust to ensure the preservation of this significant building for posterity.

Ship's Inn

89 Harbour Road, Warwick

This tiny 19th century building on the edge of Darrell's Wharf, next to a ferry stop, was given to the Bermuda National Trust in 1992 by sisters Adrianna Goodfellow and Shirley Mulder in memory of their mother. Sitting on a plot of just 0.053 of an acre, it started life as a wharf and storehouse for the Darrell family who lived at Harmony Hall (now Blackburn Place) on the opposite side of Harbour Road, although the building is much changed from its early days. Alfred Blackburn Smith bought the property in 1905 from Eliza Beltt Darrell. She was a daughter of the famous Captain Nathaniel Darrell, also known as Beau Nat, of Harmony Hall. His dining table now graces the dining room at Waterville.

Family members remember swimming by Ship's Inn, but it was never really a bathing house. In 1958 it was subdivided from the main house and came into the sole possession of Frances (Frankie) Zuill, one of AB Smith's daughters, and it was her daughters who gave it to the Trust.

One of the most interesting phases of the history of the property was the period in which Mrs AB Smith ran a Women's Work Exchange from the building. The Women's Exchange movement began in Scotland in the first half of the 19th century and developed into an international movement. These were commercial operations run by and for women selling fine needlework and handicrafts, with the goal of offering the consigners a fair source of income and the ability to work at home using traditional female skills.

During the 1930s the building became a real estate office, and in the 1950s a restaurant known as Ship's Inn. Since 1979 it has again operated as a real estate office. The building sustained damage in Hurricane Fabian in 2003, and the western sea wall was replaced soon after.

Cluster Cottage

37 St Mary's Road, Warwick
Grade I Listed Building

Cluster Cottage is an early 18th century house which survives remarkably unaltered as an excellent example of early Bermuda domestic architecture. Parts of the house could date from as early as the 17th century. It sits in two acres of grounds with fine gate posts, sturdy garden walls, a wooden porch and windows positioned close under the eaves. All the rooms have tray ceilings, joined at each corner with a natural cedar knee. The oldest part of the building is the northern chimney wing, while the main east/west section is early 18th century. There is an old mounting block near the front gate. It is believed that the cellar space beneath the cottage was used as the slaves' living quarters.

The 1898 Savage map names the property as Cluster Cottage but before that it was known as Shaddock Grove. As far as its history has been traced, the property has been in the possession of the Frith-Smith-Hutchings Presbyterian group of east Warwick and west Paget families. The house was owned by Thomas Lea Smith, an elder in Christ Church Warwick, in the mid 19th century, and descended to Alfred Blackburn Smith, who died in 1934. In 1950 his daughter Frances Adrianna (Frankie) Zuill sold it to Peter Fish.

Peter Stuyvesant Fish bore the names of the 17th century Dutch Governor of New Amsterdam (later New York) and his descendant Hamilton Fish, a close ally of Alexander Hamilton and a hero in the American Revolution. Fish's wife Florence was a sculptress, daughter of the noted artist Clark Voorhees. In 1977 Peter Fish sold Cluster Cottage to the Bermuda National Trust, which immediately let it on a long lease with protective covenants. Although the Trust could not afford to own the property at the time, the lease enabled the Trust to protect this charming home with its classic chimneys, thick walls and traditional Bermuda roof.

Tivoli

45 Middle Road, Warwick
Grade 2 Listed Building

Tivoli is a Victorian house which stands on top of a hill looking south over Middle Road in Warwick. It is a notable and highly visible example of elegant domestic architecture of the 1840s. It was built by Sanders Frith of Cedar Hill in Warwick for his son John, a doctor. Tivoli has handsome pilasters, exposed eaves and an octagonal entrance hall. The property itself spans more than 11 acres and includes the Higgs Nature Reserve to the south with a late 19th century building which may have been a grocery store.

Dr Frith's widow Emily inherited the house, and in 1872 she sold it to Christian Loblein, a native of Germany. He had arrived in the island accidentally and was recruited to serve as Bandmaster of the Bermuda Regiment. He liked Bermuda and stayed for about 40 years until he died at Tivoli in 1879. In 1890 Loblein's son Ernest sold Tivoli to TJ Wadson, who was later to become the Speaker of the House of Assembly. Wadson didn't live there, so it must have been rented out.

In 1911 Stanley Higgs, who described himself as a merchant's clerk, bought Tivoli from Wadson. In 1920 his daughter Gloria was born at Tivoli. She and her two older siblings inherited the property when their father died in 1942 and she eventually became sole owner. She lived at Tivoli all her life, maintaining the property as a working farm until she died. She was an accountant and before going to work every day she would milk all her cows by hand.

Gloria Higgs left Tivoli to the National Trust on her death in 1984, intent on protecting her beloved farmland as she witnessed the encroachment of development around her. The Trust has leased Tivoli to two schools in succession. The meadows where Miss Higgs' cows once grazed are now filled with play equipment and young children at play.

Springfield

29 Somerset Road, Sandys
Grade 1 Listed Building

The history of Springfield was researched in detail by Dr Michael Jarvis and this has set the pattern and identified sources for subsequent research of most of the National Trust's properties. Like Waterville, the Springfield estate remained the property of one family until it was purchased by the Historical Monuments Trust.

The founder of the Springfield estate, Edward Hinson, was on the property by 1662. In his time there was a substantial two-storey post and plaster house with a thatched roof and outbuildings. He died in 1676, leaving the house to his five sons. Eventually his fourth son Benjamin became the sole owner of the estate, leaving it to his daughter Mary when he died in 1715. She and her husband Ephraim Gilbert raised their 11 children there. Ephraim became important in the local Sandys Militia and prospered in his business dealings. It was during their lifetime, in the 1740s, that the original building disappeared and the main part of today's stone house was built, a small six-roomed structure.

Ephraim Gilbert died in 1769, leaving Springfield to his eldest son Thomas, who built on his father's success in both business and the Militia. Thomas' daughter Mary and her husband Thomas Hunt inherited next, leaving Springfield to their son Thomas II and his wife Susannah in 1787. They devoted much of their lives to enlarging the house and making it more modern and elegant, adding rooms, the courtyard, slave houses, a kitchen and the unusual smooth-roofed buttery for which Springfield is known. By 1827, the family had 19 slaves, including a stonemason, a ship's carpenter, labourers, house servants and three children, all living in the small, low-ceilinged outbuildings.

In the 1800s successive generations of the Gilberts died childless and the house passed to a cousin, Henry Hunt Gilbert of St George's. Henry's financial problems led him to mortgage the property, placing a financial burden on the family who eventually were no longer able to take care of it. He died in 1911, leaving the house to his children, the last of whom, Eliza, died in 1961 at Springfield, which by then had deteriorated considerably.

In 1956 the front rooms of the house were leased to the Somerset branch of the Bermuda Library. Following a restoration of the house by renowned Bermudian architect Wil Onions in 1966, the Historical Monuments Trust bought the house. Finding a use for the building proved difficult and it continued to deteriorate. The solution came from the Bermuda Government in the form of a long lease on the property to house the Sandys Community Centre. The Government renovated the property and continues to maintain it, keeping it open to the public.

Springfield had extensive grounds, part of which still remain with the house and part of which are now the Gilbert Nature Reserve. [See page 100.]

The Keep, Royal Naval Dockyard

Ireland Island, Sandys
Grade 1 Listed Building

When the American Revolution deprived Britain of access to the ports of its former colonies on the eastern seaboard of North America, it soon became obvious that Bermuda was ideally located to connect the British possessions in Canada and the West Indies. In 1795 a base was commissioned at St George's, and in 1809 the Royal Navy acquired Ireland Island in the west end for the creation of a dockyard which would become the main British naval base in the western North Atlantic.

The function of naval dockyards such as those at Gibraltar and Malta was essentially a civilian one: to repair and re-arm ships, to supply them with food, gunpowder and everything else they required as they patrolled the seas to protect the growing British Empire.

Building such a complex in Bermuda became important to the local economy, and more than 1,000 Bermudians were employed in these civilian capacities at the height of operations in the 19th century. Because these functions were so critical to the fleet, they were surrounded by heavy fortifications. In Bermuda, the fortifications surrounded the Dockyard on three sides, with the major fort of the Keep at the northern end.

The first building constructed in the Keep was the Commissioner's House (pictured right). Designed as a prototype for buildings which would withstand the inhospitable climates of naval stations around the globe, a cast iron structural frame was fabricated in England and shipped to Bermuda for assembly. This sturdy construction, combined with hard Walsingham limestone, made Commissioner's House a building that could withstand virtually anything. This experimental building is believed to have been the first use of prefabricated cast iron in domestic architecture.

Much of the Dockyard was built with convict labour, and more than 9,000 convicts were brought to Bermuda and housed in ships' hulks. During the yellow fever epidemic of 1853, over 2,000 of them died here and were buried on Watford Island (see page 72). In 1863 the last of the convicts were sent home or to Australia.

The Keep saw service through two world wars in the 20th century, and was decommissioned in 1951 when it was bought by the Government of Bermuda. For many years it was left to deteriorate, along with other buildings in the Dockyard. In 1974 Dr Jack Arnell and Andrew Trimingham, leading a committee of the National Trust, succeeded in their campaign to convert the Keep into a maritime museum. The Government leased the Keep to the National Trust for 99 years, and the Trust has leased it to the Bermuda Maritime Museum.

The Museum is now an internationally respected Bermuda institution under the direction of Dr Edward Harris, whose crowning achievement has been the meticulous and elegant restoration of the Commissioner's House.

The Architectural Heritage Project

Courtesy of Major PLA Savage RE

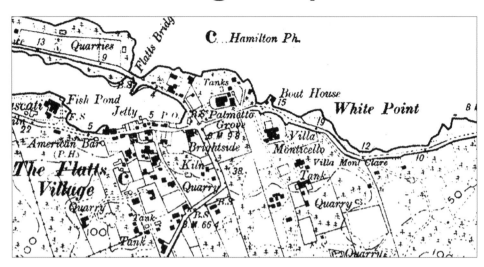

Much of the information in the preceding pages grew out of a remarkable Bermuda National Trust project started 30 years ago. In 1978 Joyce Hall, then Chair of the Trust's Buildings Preservation Committee, arranged for Professor Carl Feiss, an historical consultant from the University of Florida, to visit Bermuda. He pointed out that if the Trust was ever going to be an effective advocate for the preservation of Bermuda's architectural heritage a baseline study was needed. The project took time to get started, but in 1985 Andrew Trimingham, then President of the Trust, and John Adams, Historic Buildings Committee Chair, launched a survey of Bermuda's buildings. The guide was the Savage map, an accurate and clear record of the island prepared in 1898-9 (published 1901) by Lieutenant AJ Savage of the Royal Engineers (pictured above). It showed every building then standing in Bermuda.

Over the next ten years the project was taken forward, first by Trust Properties Officer Sylvia Shorto and then by Rosemary Clipper and Margaret Lloyd assisted by a host of fellow volunteers. Every site on which a building was recorded in 1898-9 and where something still stood in 1984 was visited, some 4,000 properties in all. Photographs were taken and a record created, including historic details as available. Rosemary Clipper compiled a computer database of the survey information which has proved to be an invaluable record during times of rampant development.

The question arose of what to do with the information. Simple publication of the data would not have been useful, as many of the buildings were too changed to be of further interest. The decision was made to identify the best surviving buildings in each parish and research them further, and feature them in a series of books, parish by parish. Margaret Lloyd has spearheaded this project from its inception. John Adams, by then the Government Archivist, was able to guide the volunteer research teams as they dug more deeply into the records than had ever been done before. The first book was *Devonshire*, written by Andrew Trimingham. *St George's* followed, written by Michael Jarvis, then still a doctoral student at William and Mary University in Virginia. This volume was used extensively when Bermuda applied to the United Nations Educational Scientific and Cultural Organisation for St George's to be designated a World Heritage Site. *Sandys* was next, followed by *Hamilton Parish* and *Smith's Parish*, which were both written by Diana Chudleigh, one of the original surveyors. Paget will follow, written by David L White. At the time of writing Pembroke is being researched, leaving only Warwick and Southampton to follow.

The books have uncovered a wealth of information which is presented in a form accessible to all. It is hoped that this will help Bermudians long into the future to appreciate their unique architectural heritage.

CHAPTER 2

HISTORIC CEMETERIES

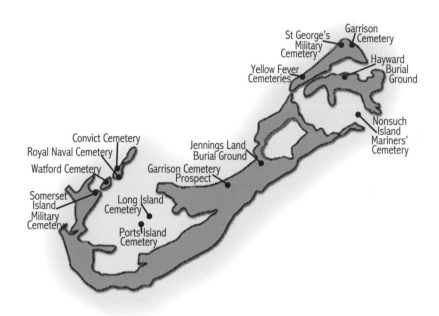

Bermuda is fortunate to have so many well-tended historical cemeteries, thanks to the Bermuda National Trust and the individuals who look after them with such dedication. Here lie the remains of admirals and shopkeepers, sailors from across the world, soldiers of the British Empire, prisoners of war, diplomats, governesses, masons and mothers, "black, white and other"; all are represented in these graveyards. In the military cemeteries are the graves of those who were sent to Bermuda from all over the world, who contributed something, however small, to making the country what it is today, and who died before they could return to their homeland. A few were famous, most had stories to tell, some barely lived at all.

These burial grounds merit recognition and protection as green spaces as well as historic monuments freely accessible to all. They are vulnerable to damage, both natural and human. Already the only record remaining of the people interred in one military cemetery, apart from the remaining few Commonwealth War Graves, are the Royal Engineer's plans 'buried' in the Archives. People who had relatives laid to rest there can no longer visit their graves. It is our moral responsibility to preserve the memorials which remain.

Far from finding them sad, gloomy places, many people enjoy the cemeteries. Some come as regular walkers who have grown to love the peaceful spaces amid the busy environment of Bermuda, others just come across them accidentally and become engrossed in reading the memorials — young men lying so far from home, families devastated by disease or disasters at sea.

Planned maintenance is vitally important and the Trust's belief in regular upkeep — supported by the Bermuda Government, the Commonwealth War Graves Commission and the West End Development Corporation — makes these beautiful graveyards accessible to all who care to venture into them. The dignity of the Victorian memorials, the life-size military accoutrements, the ship, the rock and the lambs, are kept in good repair through the dedication of individual craftsmen, despite hurricanes and vandalism. Memories of days gone by are kept alive in the inscriptions: sailors who fell from aloft, mothers who died in childbirth, prisoners who grew sick on the prison hulks. The cemeteries are also host to Bermuda's wildlife, offering a refuge in a built-up environment. These are places of reflection, spaces for life, sanctuaries for the 21st century.

Hilary Tulloch

Garrison Cemetery

Cemetery Hill

Samson's grave at Cemetery Hill

The Monuments Trust and National Trust have long cared for cemeteries as both historic sites and open spaces. In 2002, Hilary and Richard Tulloch began an exhaustive effort to record the headstones and memorials of all the graves in the Trust's care. They also researched the history of each cemetery and their report *Died at Bermuda* is the basis for much of this chapter. Most of the military cemeteries are leased to the Trust by the Bermuda Government. For many years the maintenance work in the cemeteries was supervised by honorary wardens. Michael Woods was the first and when he retired he was ably succeeded by Andrew Bermingham.

Garrison Cemetery   Grenadier Lane, St George's

This 1.66-acre walled cemetery on the eastern shore of St George's was primarily a cemetery for yellow fever victims. It was part of the St George's Garrison, the earliest establishment of the British Army in Bermuda. There are 256 memorial sites and the names of 539 individuals appear on the memorials. The majority of the deaths they record occurred during the yellow fever epidemics of 1830-1870. The three main monuments are for the yellow fever victims of the Royal Artillery, the Royal Sappers & Miners and the Queen's Regiment. This graveyard was closed in 1870 when the new military cemetery on Cemetery Hill was opened.

Grenadier Lane, on which the cemetery is located, is named for the 2nd Battalion of the Grenadier Guards. The Battalion was banished to Bermuda in 1890 and 1891 for insubordination. London was "too hot to hold them" according to the *New York Times*, which also reported that the troops were so unhappy about the heat in Bermuda that further instances of insubordination occurred. Whatever the circumstances of their exile, the presence of the Grenadiers provided the chance for a year of extravagant entertainment, receptions and balls. HRH Prince George, who later became King George V, visited Bermuda during this time, a cause for even more celebration on the island.

St George's Military Cemetery, Cemetery Hill   Secretary Road, St George's

This beautiful graveyard overlooks Murray's Anchorage on the North Shore. It is actually a set of four graveyards: a military cemetery, and a civilian cemetery divided into sections for the three Christian churches – Roman Catholic, Anglican and Methodist. Bermuda stone walls were erected to separate the two cemeteries, but some military graves ended up on the wrong side of the wall, and there are also civilian graves just inside the entrance to the military section. The entire hillside is a peaceful place away from the bustle and buzz of daily life. The land was acquired by the British Admiralty in 1868 for a military graveyard because the Garrison Cemetery had become overcrowded. Military memorials from 1853 along the adjoining wall of the civilian cemetery indicate that it was used as a military graveyard for yellow fever victims prior to its purchase.

One of the most significant graves is that of Scotsman George MacKenzie Samson, VC. Petty Officer Samson was the first Royal Naval Reserve rating to be awarded the Victoria

Garrison Cemetery

Cemetery Hill

Hayward Burial Ground

Hayward Burial Ground

Hayward Burial Ground

Cross, Britain's highest award for gallantry, at Gallipoli, Turkey, in 1915. Born in Carnoustie, Angus, in 1889, Samson was passing Bermuda while serving on a merchant ship when he developed pneumonia and died upon landing. Samson was given a full military funeral procession through St George's and was buried on 23 February 1923.

The cemetery forms part of the land which was at one point allocated to the Colonial Secretary, the administrative role that linked colonial Bermuda and London. The post came with 50 acres of farmland and Secretary Road cuts through the middle of it.

Yellow Fever Cemeteries   Ferry Road, St George's

After the yellow fever epidemic of 1853, the British garrison kept about half its soldiers encamped at Ferry Point. These two cemeteries are located in Ferry Point Park. The smaller one, Ferry Point Military Cemetery, now stands simply as a small walled area, with no visible memorials. There is evidence that there were several headstones in the 1950s but the Tullochs believe they were relocated to the Grenadier Lane cemetery. In 1782 barracks had been built near the site of the Ferry Point cemetery and the walled area was where livestock had been kept. It had varied uses over the years: it was the site of a cockfight in 1785, a cemetery by the early 19th century and later it became a garden.

The eastern cemetery, Ferry Reach Military Cemetery, was established later and may have been a result of both the Ferry Point cemetery being full due to the high death rate of the 56th Regiment, and a growing awareness that it was better to locate yellow fever cemeteries further away from places of habitation. It has a large cross and two other memorials to commemorate soldiers from the 2nd Battalion 2nd Queen's Royal Regiment who died during the yellow fever epidemic of 1864.

This area of Bermuda was once the main route for people and goods travelling from St George's to the mainland. A ferry crossing was established in the 1600s, which connected St George's to Coney Island. Since the building of the causeway in 1871, this area has become somewhat deserted.

Hayward Burial Ground   Emily's Bay Lane, St David's

This small family graveyard lies at the back of Bay House. The gift of Howard Smith, the graveyard is surrounded by an old wall and contains a few raised tombs and some attractive inscribed plaques in memory of members of the Hayward family.

Two of the graves are thought to be those of Martha Hayward and her husband Lieutenant William Lang. Lang served with the 46th Regiment of Foot under Lord Cornwallis in the American Revolution. Bermuda legend has it that when he was stationed in Bermuda he had business with Anthony Hayward and when he went to visit him, he was struck by the beauty of Hayward's daughter Martha. It was love at first sight and without her father's knowledge they married in St George's at St Peter's Church, returning later to her home to seek forgiveness. Lang is credited with bringing the first peach seeds from Madeira and there is a large peach tree growing over the western side of the graveyard to this day.

Cemetery Hill

The Yellow Fever Cemetery, Ferry Point, St George's

Mariners' Cemetery, Nonsuch Island

Nonsuch Island Mariners' Cemetery   Nonsuch Island

Nonsuch Island is only accessible by boat, with permission, as the island is a protected nature reserve. This small cemetery in the centre of the island has been used over the years by the island's inhabitants. Between 1865 and 1910 Nonsuch served as a yellow fever quarantine station and hospital, and the cemetery was established in that time. The island was a marine research station for a few years, and later a home for delinquent boys. In 1963, Dr David Wingate took up residence as the island's Warden, and began the process of re-establishing Bermuda's native flora and fauna, making Nonsuch the living museum it is today. Those interred on Nonsuch have included members of the military, sailors, scientists and, sadly, Anita Wingate, Dr Wingate's first wife and the second staff person hired by the Bermuda National Trust. Many of the graves are no longer visible. In 2000 cedar fencing was put up to enclose the greatest concentration of the graves, many of which would have been marked with simple wooden crosses that have disintegrated over time.

Nonsuch Island

Jennings Land Burial Ground   Jennings Road, Smith's

A small ancient burial ground overlooking the North Shore near Flatts, Jennings Land Burial Ground was given to the Historical Monuments Trust in 1953 by three daughters of farmer Thaddeus Trott who owned 78 acres of land in the area. The deeds refer to the burial ground as belonging to the family 'Jennyns'. The Jennings family were prominent in Bermuda in the 17th century and the Norwood survey of 1663 shows the land on which the tombs stand as belonging to Richard Jennings. The burial ground today has two unmarked stone graves and it is not known which members of the family were buried in them.

In 1955, the Monuments Trust carried out a restoration of the site. They cleared the land, restored the graves and erected a rustic fence. We have no way of knowing how faithful the grave restoration was to the original monuments. Today both graves have rather primitive headstones, one almost cruciform and the other semi-circular. It is believed there had been more grave markers and tombs during an earlier period; one eye-witness described an open vault visible in 1939. This area stands as a relic of the days when burial grounds were on family land.

Mariners' Cemetery, Nonsuch Island

Garrison Cemetery Prospect   Greenwich Lane, Devonshire

This cemetery was used first by the British Army and subsequently by the Bermuda Police Service. When the British Government was carrying out a major expansion of Bermuda's fortifications in the 1840s, it was decided that the Garrison in St George's was not ideally located and a 'flying camp' was needed to enable troops quick access to any part of the island in an emergency. The Government requisitioned large areas of Devonshire and Pembroke for Fort Prospect, Fort Hamilton and Fort Langton. Fort Prospect and the military cemetery were located on what was previously known as White Hill. Between 1840

Three views of Garrison Cemetery Prospect

and 1868, the camp at White Hill (later Prospect) was temporary, with soldiers living in tents and wooden huts. The first permanent structure was a military hospital built in 1868 to look after patients with yellow fever and typhoid, two illnesses which plagued the troops in Bermuda.

The graves date from 1866 but it is believed the land was not consecrated until 1888. The cemetery was last used by the military in 1966, and there is also a modern burial ground for police officers within the cemetery. At the rear of the cemetery, surrounded by an iron railing, lie the monument and grave of Sir Walter Kitchener, Governor of Bermuda 1908-1912, who died of appendicitis while in office.

Long Island Cemetery   Long Island, Great Sound

Long Island, Boer Memorial

Long Island Cemetery, in the middle of Hamilton Harbour, is one of the few historic cemeteries owned outright by the Trust having been donated by Government in 1972. It is, in fact, three cemeteries. The earliest is a small enclosure on the west side with two graves of men from HMS *Forth* which date from 1817.

In 1854, the Royal Naval Cemetery at Ireland Island was reaching capacity, and Long Island became the main burial ground for yellow fever victims. In 1855 it was decided that it would also be used to inter convicts. The earliest extant headstone referring to yellow fever is dated 1856, and there are many graves commemorating yellow fever victims in 1864, including Marines and workers from Boaz Island. Two doctors, 'poor Gallagher and Richards' who died trying to help the victims, are also thought to be buried here, although there is a memorial at the Royal Naval Cemetery to these two men.

The cemetery was later used for Boer prisoners of war who died while they were held captive in Bermuda on other islands in the Great Sound 1899-1902. The hospital which served these internees was on Ports Island. Their graves are marked only by a number corresponding with the main obelisk in the centre of the graveyard. There are 40 names on the obelisk which was erected by the survivors while they were awaiting repatriation. In 1903 the 56th Regiment built a stone wall to enclose the graveyard, and it was dedicated at that time by the Bishop of Newfoundland and Bermuda.

Over the years the care of these island cemeteries has been, logistically and with much hard physical work, supported by Long Island neighbours, David Lines and, more recently, Jim Butterfield.

Ports Island Cemetery   Ports Island, Hamilton Harbour

Gregg's marker at Ports Island

This small cemetery lies on the northeastern part of this large island in the Great Sound. The island itself was bought by the Admiralty Board in 1809 at the same time as the purchase of Ireland Island. The island was used to house the sick from 1816 until 1818 when the Royal Naval Hospital was built at the Dockyard. In 1834 the island was designated a Naval Quarantine Station where ships arriving in Bermuda were directed if there was sickness among the crew, as in the case of the *Pearl* which arrived with yellow fever on

Long Island Cemetery

Somerset Island

board in 1837. Convalescing convicts were sent there in 1843, and in 1852 *L'Armide*, a French hospital ship, came up from the West Indies with yellow fever. Of the 46 people who landed on the island, 11 died and are buried here. In 1853 another outbreak of the disease hit soldiers of the Royal Artillery and the 56th Regiment. Those who died are buried at Ports Island, along with the sergeant who had nursed them and several of his family. Further yellow fever deaths occurred in 1856, 1863, 1864 and 1869. In 1873 the *Doris* brought 40 cases of typhoid from Barbados.

From 1901 until 1903 the island was the location of a prison hospital 'under canvas' for the Boer War prisoners, although those who died were buried in the Boer Cemetery on Long Island. The island was also used to incarcerate German prisoners of war during the First World War.

Five graves or monuments are still visible. One commemorates the dead of the Artillery and 56th Regiment, one the crew of the *Armide* and one the grave of an eight-year-old boy. There is one further headstone with no visible inscription. In 2004 Hilary and Dick Tulloch uncovered the grave of Gunner James Gregg (pictured page 68), a victim of yellow fever from HMS *Terror* in 1864. Because of the overgrown state of the land around the cemetery area, they think it likely that further memorials may yet be discovered.

Somerset Island Military Cemetery   Mangrove Bay Road, Somerset

Somerset Island Cemetery is located on Sugar Cane Point in a bend on the road to Dockyard. The so-called "new military cemetery at Somerset" was consecrated in 1905. There are only 21 visible graves but records indicate that many more people are buried at this site. The cemetery is a tranquil 2.25-acre spot looking out to Mangrove Bay.

The earliest remaining memorial is dated 1904 and the most recent 1918. Of the 21 visible graves, 12 of the headstones are Commonwealth War Graves Commission headstones commemorating soldiers who died during the Great War, 1914-1918. The National Trust erected a small wall around the cemetery in 1986 which helps to mark the area.

Nearby there is a monument to the memory of soldiers from the 4th Battalion British West Indies Regiment, who died in Bermuda of pneumonia in 1916; it used to be next to a small chapel which has since been demolished.

Convict Cemetery   Cochrane Road, Ireland Island South

This small cemetery is hidden behind a row of former Dockyard employee houses. A tranquil spot on the northern shore, it has nine visible graves of which only five have inscriptions. The graves all date from 1843 to 1848 and two of the men whose names are still visible are known to have been convicts at the time of their death. The first convicts were brought to Bermuda from England in 1824 on HMS *Antelope* and the cemetery dates from about this time, but there is no evidence that it was ever consecrated. We know that by 1898 however, the cemetery was no longer used as cartographer Lieutenant AJ Savage marked it 'disused' on his survey map of that year.

West Indies Regiment Monument

Somerset Island Military Cemetery

Convict Cemetery

Royal Naval Cemetery

Royal Naval Cemetery   Ireland Island, Sandys

This large Naval cemetery, 2.7 acres at the side of the road leading into Dockyard, was known as the Glade. Ireland Island was bought by the Royal Navy in 1809 and the cemetery consecrated in 1812. The first burial ground was a narrow strip which is now the central portion of the cemetery; it was enlarged several times, notably after three yellow fever epidemics in 1837, 1843 and 1853. As the cemetery filled up, the categories of people who could be buried there were reduced, starting with the exclusion of convicts in 1849. By 1853 only Royal Naval personnel and residents of Ireland Island could be interred there. The third of January 1854 was marked as a day of thanksgiving in Bermuda for those who survived that dreadful scourge. It was not the last yellow fever epidemic but by 1884 the mosquito-borne disease had claimed its last victim in Bermuda.

The cemetery lies in a depression, with the earliest graves at the lower centre, and the later graves on the rising ground around them. Five admirals are buried here, as well as children and sailors. The oldest gravestone now legible is that of Sergeant John Kitchener, late Royal Marines, who died in 1816 with its cautionary verse urging the onlooker to prepare to meet his God. Several of the older headstones have poetic inscriptions, some personal and others supplied by stonemasons as far afield as Nova Scotia and England. In contrast are the Commonwealth War Graves Commission headstones which stand out in their stark simplicity. The cemetery contains the graves of servicemen from the Second World War, when Bermuda was a transit point in the Battle of the Atlantic, and memorials to some of those who were buried at sea. Overlooking the whole cemetery is the Oration Stand, a reproduction of the original structure from which the funeral oration, or formal speech at a funeral was given.

Watford Cemetery   Watford Island, Sandys

This is a small cemetery created on Watford Island in 1887 as a graveyard for soldiers and their families. Earlier in the century the whole island had been used as a burial ground for the dead of the army of convict labour that built Dockyard between 1824 and 1863. They lived in rotting hulks of ships moored just offshore, in crowded and filthy conditions; the mortality rate from dysentery and yellow fever was high. Convicts were buried in the Glade, Ireland Island until 1849 when it seemed to be filling up. Then Watford Island was used to bury dead convicts and convict officers. In 1855 it was reported that the island had received 458 bodies and was almost full. For the remaining years of convict labour those who died were buried on Long Island. Perhaps because their graves were usually marked with wooden crosses, tablets commemorating individual convicts are rare.

In 1925 the remaining few memorials were taken from other parts of the island and placed together along the north-eastern wall of the military cemetery. On 5 November 2004 the remains of five men, found exposed after Hurricane Fabian, were reburied in a single grave within the walled cemetery. The military memorials date from 1888 to 1899, with the addition in 1980 of the Queen's Regiment monument of 1866, relocated from Boaz Island. The burials included several children and four young Grenadier guardsmen who died in 1890 or 1891 during the 2nd Battalion's year-long stay.

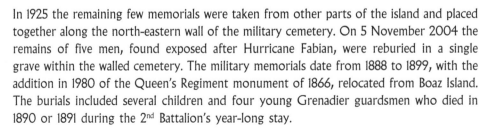

Watford Cemetery

Royal Naval Cemetery

Royal Naval Cemetery

Dr David Wingate

Dr David Wingate is Bermuda's pre-eminent conservationist, a man who has devoted his life to preserving Bermuda's environment, flora and fauna. The natural world has been his passion since he was a small child. As a young student in the 1940s he was nicknamed 'Bird' and teased by fellow students and teachers; being interested in wildlife was not exactly 'cool' at the time. At the age of 16 he was invited to join Dr Robert Cushman Murphy and Louis S Mowbray as they looked for evidence that the Cahow still nested in Bermuda. In 1968 Louis Mowbray retold the story, and described this invitation as "encouragement to a youngster who showed a marked interest in birds". In 1951 they found a Cahow sitting on her nest on one of the tiny islets of Castle Harbour where the nocturnal seabirds, presumed extinct, had been living secretly for centuries. The islands were immediately declared sanctuaries, and David Wingate has never looked back.

With a Bacheolor of Science degree from Cornell University, he returned to Bermuda and went to work for the Government. Following the rediscovery of the Cahow, a conservation project had been launched to secure the future of the species, and that is where David was focused. Cahows nest in ground burrows, placing them in heavy competition with the Bermuda Longtail. David helped to design a baffle which allowed the Cahow access to the nest, but kept out the slightly larger Longtail. This was the necessary breakthrough, and it enabled the Cahow population to grow under David's watchful eye. He removed predators, created new nesting burrows and hand-reared chicks when necessary. He also embarked on a lifelong project to recreate the world the Cahow had occupied before human settlement of Bermuda, the Living Museum of Nonsuch Island.

Nonsuch Island, 14 acres at the eastern entrance of Castle Harbour, was, like the rest of Bermuda, denuded of its cedars. Starting in 1963, David planted thousands of native plants, dug ponds and restored habitats. He reintroduced to Bermuda the Yellow-crowned Night Heron and the West Indian Topshell. He even imported the endemic White-eyed Vireo from the Bermuda mainland, as it had become island-adapted and unable to fly very far. The Bermuda Government made David the Warden of Nonsuch in 1966 when he was appointed to the newly created role of Government Conservation Officer, a job he held until his retirement in 2000.

David was one of the trustees of the Bermuda Historical Monuments Trust and President of the Bermuda Audubon Society at the time when the two organisations were working to create the Bermuda National Trust. Since its first meeting in 1970, he has been a member of the National Trust Council. He chaired the Trust's Open Space Committee from its inception and devoted himself to securing wetlands and woodlands for conservation in care of the Trust or Audubon. When the Trust was formed in 1970 it inherited part of Paget Marsh from the Monuments Trust. The remaining 240 acres described in the following chapter have been acquired since then, most of them with the involvement of David Wingate.

He has guided the Trust in what to acquire and how to care for it. Every decision starts with David's field research and relies on his judgment. He has led the Trust through the creation of new wetland habitats — Bermuda is one of the few places in the world where wetlands are actually on the increase — and woodland conservation programmes. Through it all, David has been both the man with the vision and the man on the ground doing the physical work. Not content with this, he has personally given the Trust a six-acre woodland reserve at Elm Lodge.

David Wingate is recognised in Bermuda and well beyond its shores as having done more than any other individual to preserve Bermuda's natural heritage. He has lectured and been published extensively on the Cahow and Nonsuch Island projects, and has been the subject of film documentaries and TV programmes, at home and internationally.

CHAPTER 3

PROTECTED OPEN SPACE

When I was growing up in the 1940s the whole of Bermuda was like one big national park with the people living *in* it, so it is hardly surprising that there were no formally established parks or reserves before the 1950s. Those that were established by the Government after 1950 were created in an *ad hoc* way, mainly on the British military lands that were handed back to Bermuda when the garrisons withdrew after the Second World War. Some were created in the process of reforesting scenic roadside overlooks after the devastating cedar scale epidemic, while others provided beach access for the general public. But it was not until the passage of the National Parks Act in 1986 that Bermuda's parks acquired legal designation.

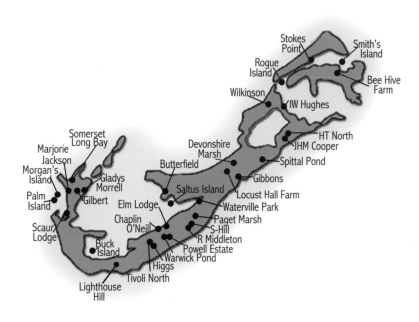

Long before then, however, the Bermuda Historical Monuments Trust and the Bermuda Audubon Society had begun protecting open spaces. When the Bermuda National Trust was set up, it became even more successful at acquiring some of our most significant and beautiful natural areas. Since 2003, in the face of ever-increasing development, the Trust and Audubon have accelerated efforts to ensure dwindling open space is protected. This powerful partnership is known as the 'Buy Back Bermuda' initiative.

Altogether, during its almost 40 years of existence, the Trust has inherited or acquired 33 properties totalling 240 acres. This network of reserves includes some of the largest and most spectacular wetlands and woodlands in Bermuda. Some, like Paget Marsh and Warwick Pond, have been enhanced for educational purposes with interpretive nature trails and a boardwalk.

Just as our historic buildings programme is intended to preserve our architectural and cultural heritage, the nature reserve system is designed to preserve and maintain Bermuda's unique natural heritage of geologic landforms and its native flora and fauna. Unfortunately, this heritage has come under increasing threat recently, not only from development outside the reserves but from an increasing host of invasive exotic species which are degrading the nature reserves themselves.

Existing resources are no longer sufficient to protect these important properties and the vital biodiversity that they host, so the National Trust is considering its next steps. Without doubt, the Trust and Buy Back need to keep acquiring these valuable open spaces before they disappear forever, but a way must be found to ensure they are rehabilitated and maintained to an appropriate standard of care. There is an urgent need for a substantial endowment to guarantee that these properties have the necessary resources directed for their care on an ongoing basis. Bermuda's open spaces and nature reserves are too important to neglect. We owe it to future generations to get this right.

David B. Wingate

Central Wetlands

RWG

Great Egret in breeding plumage

RWG

Green Heron on Mangrove prop roots

Wetlands are vitally important elements of Bermuda's ecosystem, and home to much of our share of the world's biodiversity. The majority of the surviving wetlands originally formed part of a long chain of ponds and marshes that used to stretch from Barnes Corner in Southampton to Mangrove Lake in Smith's Parish. What remains is the marshland that was not filled in by rubbish dumping, a practice that cost Bermuda many of its environmentally important pond and swamp areas. Today, each wetland area that can be saved or restored represents a victory for this delicate North Atlantic island ecology, providing habitat for migratory birds, waterfowl, freshwater fish and other wildlife species.

Bermuda was not alone in considering wetlands as little more than wasteland; this was true all over the world until the the second half of the 20th century when their importance was highlighted by a burgeoning environmental movement. This awareness led to the International Convention on Wetlands, signed in Ramsar, Iran in 1971, and now known as the Ramsar Convention. It is an intergovernmental treaty for the conservation and wise use of wetlands and their resources. At the time of writing, there were 158 contracting parties to the Convention, with 1,755 wetland sites designated for inclusion in the Ramsar List of Wetlands of International Importance – known as 'Ramsar sites'. In 1999, the first of Bermuda's wetlands were designated for the Ramsar List, with additional sites being recommended as Wetlands of International Importance in 2003 following a review of all wetlands in the UK's territories.

HT North Nature Reserve   Mangrove Lake, South Road, Smith's Parish

In 1975 the heirs of Mr and Mrs Henry Thompson North gave a portion of Mangrove Lake and an acre of land to the National Trust in memory of their parents. Over the next few years, the Trust ran a 'Save Open Spaces' fund-raising campaign and purchased a neighbouring lot, making the reserve 4.5 acres. The reserve protects an extensive stand of shoreline mangroves as well as the wooded hillside to the west.

HT North is one of the most important reserves in the Trust's care, with two critically important ecosystems – a saltwater pond and pond mangroves – as well as the upland woodland. Bermuda's saltwater ponds boast a remarkable diversity of species, second only to coral reefs. Mangrove Lake is the largest, and its size contributes both to its stability and to the variety of life it supports. It is one of only two sites where the native Diamondback Terrapin breeds, and is home to two breeding herons – the Yellow-crowned Night Heron and the Green Heron, which feeds on the endemic Bermuda Killifish. The Red Mangroves edging the western side of Mangrove Lake contribute greatly to the concentration of

Grumpy Yellow-crowned Night Heron drying its feathers after an accidental dip in Mangrove Lake

Mangrove Lake

Wild Freesias at Mangroville

biodiversity and provide shelter for many marine species such as sponges and oysters on their submerged prop roots. Mangrove Lake and Trott's Pond have been proposed for designation as Ramsar sites because they "represent Bermuda's largest enclosed brackish/salt water ponds. Around the edges are the healthy mangrove swamps. They contain unique fish, algal and invertebrate communities which differ greatly from true marine environments. They are important nesting and foraging areas for water birds."

Mangroville Cottage   11 Judkin Lane, Hamilton

Across the lane from the North Nature Reserve sits Mangroville Cottage on a 2.7-acre site, overlooking Mangrove Lake and effectively adding substantially to the land area of the reserve. It was left to the Trust in 2003 by Natalie North, a sports teacher at the Bermuda High School. Used in the 19th century as a post office, it was much altered in the 20th century, and today is leased out for residential use. The house is surrounded by a lush garden that abounds with Wild Freesias in the spring, and in the summer is shaded by an old Royal Poinciana tree. Behind the house and on the way to Arrowroot Lane are the remains of an orchard. Today it seems an odd place to have located a post office, but in those days a road ran north of the pond from Tucker's Town to Devil's Hole.

JHM Cooper Nature Reserve

JHM Cooper Nature Reserve   South Shore, Smith's Parish

This 1.7-acre reserve is located near the HT North Nature Reserve. About a quarter-acre is arable, and is leased to a farmer, while the remainder of the property comprises peat marsh with no open water. It was once trenched to create open water for *Gambusia*, the 'mosquito fish' which feed on mosquito larvae, but the ditches have long since become overgrown. Gerald Dupont Hollis, a farmer, owned this land for many years, and his widow sold it to her nephew, who in turn sold it to his sister, Elma Cooper. She died in 1970, leaving it in trust for the support and medical care of her son, John Henry Maxwell Cooper. His trustees sold off the land; since this lot was subject to a preservation agreement, it was sold to the Trust at a very generous rate in 2000.

A trail to the sea at Spittal Pond

Spittal Pond Bird Sanctuary   South Road, Smith's Parish

An oceanfront valley on the South Shore, this National Trust property forms the centre of a jointly owned nature reserve of 64 acres. The Trust owns almost 24 acres, the Spittal Pond Bird Sanctuary. The surrounding land, Spittal Pond National Park, is owned by the Bermuda Government, which leases part of it to a dairy farmer. While today it seems obvious that the public should have access to the Trust's portion of the reserve, the decision to create the first trail in 1966 came only after much debate. In the end, concern about a lack of open space, evident even at that early date, trumped the desire to retain the reserve as an undisturbed bird sanctuary. Balance was achieved by fencing off the core and laying out the trail so that visitors could see every part of the pond, without actually entering the protected area. The pond continues to be of environmental significance and was declared a Ramsar site in 1999 because it is "Bermuda's most important wetland for wintering waterfowl".

A White-tailed Tropic Bird, popularly known as a Longtail, comes in for a landing at her nest on the cliffs at Spittal Pond

Heading south -- a Stilt Sandpiper at Spittal Pond in August

The native Diamondback Terrapin which can be found at Mangrove Lake

The endemic White-eyed Vireo

Spittal Pond Nature Reserve includes five of Bermuda's six terrestrial ecosystems, ranging from upland forest to coastal salt-resistant areas. It contains the only salt marsh ecosystem in Bermuda, unique in that it is a spill-over marsh flooded by the sea in hurricanes and severe storms. This made it unappealing for development, and is why such a large piece of land in an otherwise desirable location has remained intact. The sea flooding maintains the habitat as open water and mudflats, creating a variation in salinity through the year. Few species can survive in such an environment, although those which can — such as Wigeon Grass and mosquito fish — flourish due to the high nutrient content of the water. Some 20 bird species regularly winter at Spittal Pond, while a total of 200 species have been recorded as visitors there.

The reserve also contains some excellent Bermudian geological features. Most notable is the 'checkerboard', which effectively provides a record of sea level recession from the time of the last interglacial high sea stand around 120,000 years ago. It comprises, in vertical sequence, a submarine habitat (the checkerboard itself), topped by a beach berm, and a back beach dune. The checkerboard reveals the submarine deposits left by the receding ocean. During Bermuda's whaling industry days in the 18th century, whales were hauled ashore here, and stripped of their commercially valuable blubber.

To complete the picture, Spittal Pond boasts two important historic sites, Jeffrey's Hole, a cave formation where an escaped slave concealed himself, and Spanish Rock. Originally thought to be where Spanish sailors had come ashore in the 16th century, the so-called Spanish Rock is inscribed 'RP 1543'. The RP is for 'Rex Portugalis' (King of Portugal), carved by a sailor from a Portuguese ship out of Hispaniola wrecked off Bermuda's north shore. In the 1920s a misguided effort to preserve the fast-eroding carving by enclosing it in glass actually hastened its decay. Fortunately, an American visitor had made a lead mould of the carving in 1893; in 1940 this was turned into a fine bronze cast for the site.

In spite of the awareness of its value to the people of Bermuda, it took decades actually to protect Spittal Pond for the public. Original land grants in Bermuda were north/south oriented strips of land, so acquiring the property involved a complex process of buying the ten strips that made up the area. The first piece — the eastern 4.2 acres — was bought in 1946 by the founder of the Bermuda Historical Monuments Trust, Dr Henry Wilkinson, and transferred to the National Trust in 1973. In 1956, Government purchased the North's Point headland and turned it into a roadside park. Gradually over the years, additional land was added as it became available, and in 1976 the Government transferred the strip incorporating Spanish Rock to the Trust.

The name Spittal Pond comes from its use as a hospital ('spital') for sick animals. Used as 'grazing commons' over the years, it has also been known as Brackish Pond and Peniston's Pond.

The reserve was badly damaged when it took a direct hit from Hurricane Fabian in 2003. A generous donation by Bermuda residents Richard and Helen Fraser enabled extensive restoration to take place in 2005, including removal of felled trees, excavation of the woodland pond, new fencing and trails, with interpretive signage and bird observation blinds still to come. The management objectives require that Spittal Pond serves both as a recreation area and a bird sanctuary.

The central reserve at Spittal Pond Bird Sanctuary

The king of Spittal Pond, the Yellow-crowned Night Heron

Gibbons Nature Reserve South Road, Devonshire

This 3.2-acre reserve is known for its distinctive avenue of ancient Bermuda Palmetto along the South Shore Road – possibly relics of the original pre-colonial forest. It lies in the southern section of Devonshire's two major valley configurations, forming part of a long chain of marshlands extending along the South Shore on the lee side of what were once sand dunes. Donated to the Trust in 1976 in memory of philanthropic local businessman Edmund Gibbons by his sons, former Premier Sir David Gibbons and former Mayor of Hamilton Graham Gibbons, the marsh is a sanctuary for migrating birdlife. It is an important nesting site for the Moorhen or Common Gallinule, the only species of waterfowl to remain common since Bermuda was colonised.

Formerly known as Smith's Marsh, it was once filled with sedges, rushes, Palmetto, Cedar and Wax Myrtle. People were starting to use this marsh as yet another dump site leading Edmund Gibbons to acquire it "in order to protect this beautiful section of marsh along the South Shore Road from being filled in as a garbage dump". The Trust dug out the area that had been filled, making a pond, and the Bermuda Audubon Society funded the laying of power lines underground to save birds from flying into them.

Devonshire Marsh Nature Reserves Jubilee & Vesey Streets, Devonshire

Devonshire Marsh is the northernmost of the parish's two major valley configurations. The east and west basins comprise the largest contiguous open space in Bermuda, giving the area significant aesthetic and ecological value. Containing Bermuda's largest peat marsh habitat and fresh water lens, the marsh was never used for dumping rubbish. It was, however, extensively filled around the edges with quarry waste to create farmland for growing celery, which, unusually, actually enhanced its value as habitat. This filled area later became wet pasture. When the Department of Health was carrying out its programme to control mosquitoes in the mid 20th century, ditches were dug around Devonshire Marsh to create open water areas in which the mosquito larvae-eating *Gambusia*, the mosquito fish, could flourish. This also added to the habitat value, although today the ditches have become overgrown with the invasive cattail. Unlike some of the peat marshes, because of its brush fire prone sawgrass/bracken fern savannah, Devonshire Marsh has been extensively burned, first in the 'great fire' of 1914, and most recently in the late 1980s. But it is the wet pasture and the ditches that attract the birdlife.

Devonshire Marsh is especially notable for its diversity of marsh ferns, including the endemic Ten-Day Fern. It has been proposed as a Ramsar site because it is "Bermuda's largest peat marsh habitat, consisting of a mosaic of sawgrass swamp, bracken fern savannah, cattail, wet pasture and relic fragments of peat hammock forest. [It] provides important unfragmented habitat for local, migratory and overwintering shorebirds, waterbirds, landbirds and raptors."

The conservation history of Devonshire Marsh is one of good news and bad news. The good news is that since 1965 a great deal of this critical ecosystem has gradually been acquired by the Trust and the Bermuda Audubon Society, with the ultimate goal of

Palmettos at Gibbons Nature Reserve

The Moorhen or Common Gallinule

Gibbons Nature Reserve

The Great Egret

The Gulf Fritillary

Devonshire Marsh East

The Warwick Green Anole

The Great Egret

Dennis' Walk at Paget Marsh

retaining the entire marsh basin as a unified reserve. The first purchase by the Trust was of ten acres in the eastern basin, acquired in 1984 from the heirs of Eugenius Zuill of Loyal Hill, who was known as a very progressive farmer. In 1989 one of the Historical Monuments Trust founding members Hereward Watlington bequeathed to the Trust and Audubon nine acres in the western basin along Jubilee Road. In 1990, business leaders Sir John Cox and Sir Bayard Dill, as the surviving trustees of a charitable trust that had bought land in the area to create a playground, conveyed their 1.4-acre site in the centre of the marsh to the Trust. Audubon owns a further 14 acres of the eastern basin. This means about 35 acres is now in protective ownership.

However, despite the environmental importance of Devonshire Marsh, there is a long history of industrial encroachment into the marsh, including violations of planning regulations which threaten the hydrological integrity of the eastern basin. The 1.4-acre parcel given to the Trust in 1990 was under lease at the time to a tenant who had used it for industrial purposes for years. The Trust continues work to minimise the impact.

We are fortunate to have a delightful description of how the marsh looked in the 19th century. Laura Cox Bluck of nearby Orange Valley wrote in her diary in about 1860:

> "At the foot of our hill stretched the lovely marsh, a favourite playground of the children. The marsh was filled with giant cedars and it would take four, sometimes five children to span these trees with their little arms stretched to touch the finger tips of the other child. These cedars made an umbrella like shade so that even during a bright day it was like twilight under them. There were also many palmettos, some very old and twisted. The ground was covered with high ferns and the marshy border was fragrant with peppermints and grand mints. Stepping stones led through the marsh to the Church at the southern end and to neighbours on either side. The cedars were always full of bluebirds and their nests and singers (cicadas) singing in the warm air. Cows roamed through the marsh and in the evenings they came home perfumed with the mints through which they had trodden during the day."

Paget Marsh Nature Reserve
Middle Road, Paget

Paget Marsh is the jewel in the crown of Trust nature reserves, and has tremendous environmental and historic importance. It is the last significant tract of peat marsh swamp in Bermuda to have survived virtually unmodified by man since prehistoric times. Protected basins and inland valleys throughout Bermuda would almost certainly have looked like Paget Marsh when Sir George Somers arrived in 1609. The land would have been densely covered with Palmetto, with specimens of Bermuda Cedar breaking through the canopy to provide the straight tall trees that were vital to the shipbuilding industry and the island's economic prosperity.

It took many years to acquire the 25 acres which make up the reserve today. Dr Henry Wilkinson led the effort, purchasing property from two of the three main Paget Marsh landowners for the Monuments Trust in 1952 and 1958. Mary Gray, the third owner, bequeathed the Audubon Society the option to buy her share of the marsh at a favourable rate. They bought the property in 1965, and it became a joint venture with the Monuments

A juvenile Yellow-crowned Night Heron, proof that they breed at Paget Marsh

The Buckeye, an endemic sub-species

The Palmetto forest at Paget Marsh

Snowy Egret

Stately palms at Warwick Pond

Mother duck with her ducklings

Trust: Audubon bought the marsh and the Monuments Trust bought the adjoining agricultural land and Lammermuir Cottage. In 1975 the Society for the Prevention of Cruelty to Animals enhanced the reserve by giving the National Trust a further two acres, which they no longer needed.

Much of the 25-acre property comprises the largest remaining Cedar and Palmetto swamp in Bermuda, with the Palmettos growing closely together and forming a canopy under which some of the last small colonies of Bermuda's endemic Sedge and Wild Bermuda Pepper survive. The marsh also contains representation of all other marsh habitats in Bermuda, including a mangrove pond. The site was originally connected by caves to Hamilton Harbour, and would have begun as a tidal saltwater pond surrounded by mangroves. Over the years, the formation of peat on the marsh bottom cut off access to the ocean, isolating the mangroves and turning the marsh brackish.

Paget Marsh escaped some of the ravages that humans inflicted on other marshes, with limited dumping. Mosquito control ditches were dug around the marsh in the 1940s, making it hard to access. In addition, the acidity of its soil held off most invasive species. Two of them did thrive, however — Guava and Ardisia (Marlberry) — and by the 1970s they were threatening the sedges and ferns of the forest understorey. A successful invasive control programme was launched through the 1980s and 1990s, but since then new invasives have moved in. Global warming has posed the latest, and perhaps greatest threat to Paget Marsh. The associated exceptionally high tides have killed off hundreds of the surviving Cedar specimens, literally drowning them. Most of these trees are more than 200 years old, and they were an integral part of this prehistoric marsh environment.

In managing Paget Marsh, the National Trust and the Audubon Society have tried to balance the need to protect its unique ecosystem with the value of allowing people to visit and experience primeval Bermuda. In 1997 a wooden boardwalk was built through the marsh to enable access while reducing the impact of visitors on the forest understorey. Educational signs were also installed. At the same time, the portion of the marsh that had been used for dumping was excavated to create a pond with islands, providing habitat for resident and migratory birds. To honour their contributions to conservation in Bermuda, the pond was named for David Wingate and the boardwalk for former National Trust President Dennis Sherwin, who funded the project.

Warwick Pond Nature Reserve & the Powell Woodland

Middle Road, Warwick

Warwick Pond was bought for the Trust by Bermuda resident and environmentalist Dennis Sherwin in 1979. The adjoining Powell Woodland was purchased with the proceeds of a 2006 fund-raising gala. Together they form a 13-acre reserve in the heart of one of the most densely populated parts of Bermuda. Its environmental value is significant, and it also adds to the beauty of the area. Both of these properties had in the past been sub-divided into some 30 to 40 'voting shares', enabling the owners to live and vote in one parish, while also owning land, and the accompanying right to vote, in another parish. Once the 1968 Constitution put an end to this practice, Warwick resident Graham Powell started to

The Blue Dasher dragonfly (above) and the Rambur's Forktail damselfly (above right), both Bermuda natives and common around freshwater ponds

Warwick Pond

acquire the shares comprising the Warwick Pond property. A decade later, he offered the land to the Trust at a favourable rate. Nearly 30 years later, one of his heirs offered the neighbouring Powell Woodland to the Trust on equally generous terms.

Warwick Pond itself is the largest surviving freshwater pond in Bermuda. It was declared a Ramsar site because of its size, its importance to both resident and migratory waterfowl, and the fact that it is the only site in which the endemic Killifish has a freshwater-adapted population. The western end mudflats, which form in summer when high evaporation rates lower the water level of the pond, are rich in nutrients for migratory shorebirds. Under these conditions up to 16 species of shorebirds and plovers can be seen here, but heavy rains flooding the mudflats will quickly drive them to the golf courses. The northern end of the pond supports lush agricultural fields which are leased to a local farmer.

The wooded hillside on the eastern side of the pond, together with the Powell Woodland, form part of the extensive Allspice woodland that borders the entire length of the Warwick Railway Trail. Some of the trees are 80 feet tall, and among the largest in Bermuda. There are also a number of healthy Bermuda cedars, and in the rocky southern section the endemic Bermuda Maidenhair Fern can be found.

Because of the central location and the range of ecosystems in the reserve, the Trust has created walking trails and interpretive signage, also funded by Dennis Sherwin, who has established an endowment for the maintenance of the Warwick Pond and Paget Marsh reserves. In 2008, the Catlin End to End Committee funded trails and signage for the Powell Woodland.

Higgs Nature Reserve Middle Road, Warwick

The Tivoli property, bequeathed to the Trust in 1984 by Gloria Higgs, contains a wide variety of habitats, from upland woodland to low-lying wetland. The southern portion of the property, across Middle Road from the house and hillside, is all that remains of the Warwick West marsh, which once extended from the Warwick Post Office to the Warwick Riding Stables. Most of it was filled in by rubbish dumping in the 1960s and 1970s, but Miss Higgs held out and refused to allow the Tivoli marshland to be filled. As development grew up around it, this small reserve seemed to be disappearing. It has been saved by a generous gift from the family of the late Sir John Sharpe, a former Premier of Bermuda, which has enabled the Trust to turn this former wasteland into a gem of a nature reserve.

Improvements to the site began with the creation of a perimeter pond around the marsh edge. This isolates the central, undisturbed peaty portion of the marsh with its diverse, tall and dense marsh flora, making it a safe nesting area for marsh birds. The open water itself is appealing to migratory water birds and the mosquito fish manage the area's mosquito population. Part of the dry land will be used for grazing or fodder grass cutting, and the corner adjacent to the carpentry shop is being turned into a public park with shade trees so that visitors can comfortably observe the wildlife.

The nature reserve has been named after the donor, Gloria Higgs, and the pond is known as Jack's Pond, for 'Jack' Sharpe, as he was known.

The Yellow-crowned Night Heron

Higgs Nature Reserve

Anole lizard blowing his throat sac

Royal Palms at the Higgs Nature Reserve

Woodland Reserves

The Monarch butterfly

The woodland at Hughes Reserve

Woodlands were originally the most common habitat in Bermuda, and today they are the most threatened — both by development and invasive species. They are home to many of our native flora, they support woodland species like the endemic White-eyed Vireo or 'Chick of the Village', they create 'breathing space' in a heavily populated island, and they help to conceal the density of development. The Trust is grappling with two main issues: loss of woodland habitat to development and loss of Bermudian native forest to invasives such as Brazil Pepper. Acquiring and protecting Bermuda's woodlands is a top priority for the Trust.

Wilkinson Nature Reserve   Fractious Street, Hamilton

A steep and lushly wooded hillside, presently dominated by non-native trees such as Fiddlewood, Allspice and Chinese Fan Palm, this half-acre parcel of land was a gift from Mrs Bernard Wilkinson in memory of her husband, Henry Bernard Logier Wilkinson. She conveyed it to the Trust in 1982. Her reasons really sum up the motivation for most gifts of open space to the Trust: "for the principal purpose of promoting the well-being of bird life and as a sanctuary for birds and other wildlife, and to preserve the natural features". Being by nature cautious, she required that the Trust declare the land inalienable within two months, which the Trust Council was happy to do.

IW Hughes Nature Reserve

The Hughes reserve was partly donated by the heirs of Idwal W Hughes in 1982. Located off Harrington Sound Road and lying adjacent to the large private Walsingham Trust, the reserve represents a 1.25-acre addition to the 22 acres of the Walsingham Reserve. Like the larger reserve, it includes Bermuda's oldest geological formation. Known as the Walsingham formation, it is characterised by extensive pinnacle rocks and cave systems.

A central feature of the Hughes reserve is a fracture cave which looks like a canyon extending well below sea level. The rare native Bermuda Cave Fern grows on the cliff overhangs of the cave. Because of its 'karst' topography, making it rocky and irregular, the Walsingham tract was spared from development in earlier centuries because it was no use for farming or grazing, and could not even be used for timber extraction. The rock was also too hard to be quarried for building. As a result, much of Bermuda's rarest upland native and endemic flora survives undisturbed. The reserve features some ancient Bermuda Olivewood trees that survive from the earliest settlement days.

The Gray Catbird, a Bermuda native

Cardinal perched on Bermuda Palmetto

Butterfield Nature Reserve   Point Shares Road, Pembroke

Located in Point Shares, the reserve's entrance is marked by a set of moss covered steps and a brass plaque. The first section was given to the Trust in 1981 by Mr and Mrs Dudley Butterfield. In 1984, the day after a bulldozer appeared to excavate and demolish woodland on the adjoining half-acre lot, Mr Butterfield purchased it and added it to the Butterfield Reserve. In 2000 and 2003, the Butterfields donated a further 1.5 acres, making the entire reserve just over 2.5 acres.

By far the most important section of the property is the first piece: a steeply sloping hillside comprising an intact remnant of upland Bermuda Palmetto forest. The conveyance documents note: "…as it has been ascertained that growing on the land is an almost pure forest of endemic Bermuda Palmetto with an understorey of endemic Bermuda Sedge, the grantor has decided to make a gift of the land as a nature reserve, and the grantee has agreed to accept it on the basis of making it a nature reserve and for the preservation of the endemic flora thereon".

Some of the palmettos still bear the scars from sap-tapping; in early days palmetto sap was fermented into a highly alcoholic drink called bibby. The more recently donated sections of the reserve include a tennis court with a small changing house, two banana patches and an overgrown garden containing unusual exotic palms and Heliconia.

In its own way, the Butterfield Reserve shows as much diversity as any of the Trust properties: from ancient forest to modern gardens.

Rebecca Middleton and S-Hill Land Nature Reserves   Ord Road, Paget

These two small reserves lie on one of the most popular and scenic sections of the Railway Trail between Harmony Hall, S-Hill and the South Shore Road in Paget, and so they contribute to the 'Emerald Necklace' of Bermuda's linked open spaces.

Together about three-quarters of an acre, they comprise woodland similar to that of the Powell estate further west: mature woodland with a diverse mix of naturalised tree species and a fairly clear understorey. The first lot was a quarter-acre site donated in 1992 by Adrianna Goodfellow, who, with her sister, also gave the Ship's Inn property at Darrell's Wharf to the Trust. The second lot, 0.4 acres, was donated by Mr and Mrs Walter Cook to the Trust in 2006 and named in memory of Rebecca Middleton, the Canadian teenager who was brutally murdered at Ferry Reach in 1996. Coincidentally, Mrs Mingo Cook's maiden name is Middleton and the nature reserve is part of the area that was once owned by the Middleton family, as evidenced by the nearby Middleton Lane.

Because of their close proximity, the two reserves are managed together. The chief management challenge is the invasive Giant Balloon Vine which can quickly overwhelm mature canopy trees. In accepting these reserves, the Trust took on the challenge of controlling the vine; Warwick Academy students and other volunteer groups have helped to clear some of this and other invasives in the reserves to enable the native plants and trees to flourish.

The Bermuda Sedge

A young cedar tree at Middleton

Rebecca Middleton Nature Reserve

The Palmetto forest at Butterfield Nature Reserve

An old stone wall at the Middleton Reserve

Elm Lodge Nature Reserve

Harbour Road, Warwick

Donated by one of the Trust's founding Council members Dr David Wingate, this six-acre reserve is a significant tract of woodland, with agricultural land, pasture and an orchard. The property had been owned by the 'gentleman privateer' Hezekiah Frith, who sold it to Captain Thomas Nelmes in 1829. It stayed in the Nelmes family until the early 1970s when Laura Nelmes Pattison and her husband Pierre both died and Pierre Pattison's sister Aileen Pattison Wingate inherited. Dr Wingate's parents knew of his passion for protecting open space, and gave the property to him in 1983. In the same spirit, he gave it to the Trust. In announcing this gift, Dr Wingate said: "I am doing this because I perceive that our rapidly diminishing and fragmented woodlands are under the greatest threat by development and I want to put my money where my mouth is."

Most of the land is woodland, ideally suited to the Bermuda Cedar, as well as some interesting non-invasive imports which provide habitat for birds and other wildlife. It is to be managed as a nature reserve for research on woodland management and native forest restoration with an emphasis on Bermuda Cedar. The property also features arable land which is actively farmed, walking trails and a deep valley with a fruit orchard. Additional features are a quarry and remarkably well-preserved ancient lime kiln, which would have been used for the slow-burning of limestone to produce lime mortar for building and lime wash. This is the only lime kiln on any Trust property, and the Trust will propose its listing as an historic monument.

Looking across Granaway Deep

Chaplin O'Neill Nature Reserve

Harbour Road, Warwick

Donated by Lady Oona O'Neill Chaplin in 1989 this 0.56-acre reserve comprises a woodland area and a strip of waterfront. The property features Bermuda Palmetto and the shrub St Andrew's Cross and commands magnificent views overlooking Granaway Deep.

Eugene O'Neill, the US playwright, bought the Spithead property on Harbour Road in Warwick in 1926, taking out a $10,000 mortgage which he never paid off. In 1928, he abandoned his family — wife Agnes, daughter Oona and son Shane — promising in his divorce settlement to leave the Bermuda property to his children. But when he died in 1953 he left everything to his third wife, Carlotta Monterey, disinheriting both children. However, his daughter married in 1943 and her husband, the legendary actor Charlie Chaplin, took over the Spithead mortgage in 1951. In 1970, settlement with Ms Monterey was reached, and the property finally became Oona's.

Chaplin O'Neill Reserve

In 1987, now Lady Chaplin, Oona decided to sell the Bermuda property. She subdivided it into three lots, selling two as house sites. She donated the remaining half acre to the National Trust to become the Chaplin O'Neill Nature Reserve. The subdivision was approved subject to a conservation order, a Section 34 Agreement, which prohibited development on the hillside leading down to Harbour Road. Building permission was granted to the buyers of her property on the condition that their development would have no impact on the protected hillside. Some years later the houses were built, with access from the south. However, the owners applied to create additional access from Harbour Road, which involved cutting through the protected hillside. The application was refused four times by the

Seaside Oxeye at Chaplin O'Neill

A woodland path at Elm Lodge Reserve

Limes from the Elm Lodge orchard

Palmettos at Elm Lodge

The Golden Silk Spider

A Goldfinch in a Casuarina

Tivoli North

A big Warwick Anole at Tivoli North

Development Applications Board, but was finally approved on appeal to the Minister for the Environment. Believing that Section 34 Agreements were unbreakable conservation covenants, the Trust successfully appealed this decision to the Supreme Court. The owners then took their case to the Court of Appeal, which found in their favour overturning the earlier ruling and enabling the development to proceed. The Trust Council decided not to take it to the higher court, the British Privy Council. This series of events represented a bleak day for conservation in Bermuda. The courts had ruled that the Section 34 Agreement, previously used to protect environmentally significant parts of the island for future generations, was in fact not the watertight mechanism it should have been.

Tivoli North   45 Middle Road, Warwick

The 12-acre Tivoli property comprises valley and upland hillside habitat. It is made up of three distinct elements: the house (leased as a nursery school), the lower wetland (now the Higgs Reserve) and the hillside woodland known as Tivoli North Nature Reserve. Left to the Trust by Gloria Higgs in 1984, the estate's hillside had been a dairy farm, and grazing had denuded the property of mature vegetation.

The Trust embarked on a major reforestation project, replanting it mainly with the endemic Bermuda Cedar and Palmetto. But 25 years later invasives such as the Brazil Pepper had gained the upper hand, dominating the slower-growing Cedars and Palmettos. Another woodland management programme was instituted, with funding from the UK's Overseas Territories Environment Fund. This time the project was targeted at removing invasives to enable the native trees to become pre-eminent.

Lighthouse Hill Nature Reserve   South Road, Southampton

Early in the 21st century it became clear that conservation of Bermuda's few remaining undeveloped areas was at greater risk than ever from the pressure of increasing development. It was the downside of Bermuda's booming economy. Faced with a government proposal to build a hospital on part of the central public open space the Botanical Gardens, and the overturning of the Section 34 Agreement at the former Chaplin O'Neill property, the Trust Council's focus turned intently to a strategy of open space purchase. It had become clear that the only way to protect environmentally important land from unwanted development was to place it in the hands of conservation organisations such as the National Trust and the Bermuda Audubon Society. The Trust team sought properties of significant environmental value that were affordably priced because of conservation zoning or Section 34 Agreements. The first such purchase was the Powell Woodland (see page 86), and in 2008, another opportunity appeared and thanks to another gala fund-raiser, the Trust bought Lighthouse Hill, a valuable piece of woodland.

Lighthouse Hill is a reserve of nearly eight acres on the South Road in Southampton, directly below the Gibbs Hill Lighthouse. It results from a good example of cluster development, in which the dwelling units were grouped on one part of the site enabling a large block of open space to be retained. Its conservation significance is based on a

Lighthouse Hill Nature Reserve

number of factors: its large size; the diversity of tree species with relatively few of the worst invasives; and the low percentage of trees being lost to recent hurricanes. As an amenity to Bermuda's tourism industry, it also offers a stretch of undeveloped land right opposite major tourism facilities on South Road. The site is adjacent to recently acquired government parkland, and the two locations offer the opportunity to create a half-mile long rural pathway from the South Shore, over Lighthouse Hill to the Railway Trail. This latest addition to the Trust's portfolio of woodland reserves is of major significance to woodland conservation in Bermuda.

A Gulf Fritillary shows its underwings

Scaur Lodge Nature Reserve — Somerset Road, Sandy's

Scaur Lodge occupies a strategic scenic location at the head of the scaur, a shallow rock-strewn stretch of water set between two headlands on the southern tip of Somerset Island. It is a six-acre reserve donated in 1976 by Elsa Beatrice Mott Ives of the notably philanthropic CS Mott family from the US.

This property overlooks two Trust reserves, Morgan's Island and Palm Island in Ely's Harbour. It comprises a wooded hillside which has been planted with native tree species. The reserve falls away sharply, leading down to a small beach which was traditionally used for careening boats to clean and repair their hulls. A house on the site was badly damaged by a tornado, and after much discussion (in which it was described by the Trust's Director as "that tumble-down old building") it was demolished before the land was given to the Trust, and the ridge top was restored as a potential arable field. The original historic buttery still stands, however, although it has suffered damage from ficus roots, and there are stables on the site. There is a quarter-acre of agricultural land, and the whole reserve has a peaceful rural feeling.

Scaur Lodge arable land

Gladys Morrell Nature Reserve — Mangrove Bay, East Shore Road, Sandys

Gladys Morrell, Bermuda's leading suffragist, gave this two-acre site to the Imperial Order of the Daughters of the Empire, Sandys Chapter in 1951 "in appreciation of the spirit which has animated the Sandys chapter in carrying out the undertaking of the Order both in war time and in peace, and in the hope that the field she gives them may provide a centre for their activities in the future and give them wider scope". As Mrs Morrell wrote in her *History of the IODE in Bermuda*, the Chapter intended to build a hall on the site for their many community projects, and she hoped the field could be used for outdoor fetes or flower shows. Although Mrs Morrell reported that the building fund was up to £2,000, in the end the Daughters of the Empire felt that there were enough halls in the vicinity and they donated the land to the Trust in 1973 in memory of Gladys Morrell.

The Trust saw this as an opportunity to establish a native forest in a sheltered upland valley, well away from the salt spray. The area was mass-planted with the full range of native trees in 1974. While the new forest grew in well, the invasive species began to overwhelm the natives in the absence of sufficient funding to manage the property.

The path at Gladys Morrell

The view from Scaur Lodge

The endemic White-eyed Vireo

Bluebird nestbox at Gladys Morrell

This problem of invasives in the Trust's reserves has been a matter of growing concern. In 2004 the Gladys Morrell Nature Reserve was chosen as the first site to undergo a major reclamation project for native species. Led by Dr David Wingate and funded by the UK's Overseas Territories Environmental Programme, the project involved a significant culling of invasives and planting of native species. This effort will take several years and much vigilance to complete, as the invasives are always the first plants to colonise the cleared areas. The Trust will continue to remove the fast-growing invasives so that the slower-growing native species can establish themselves. Until they do, it will not be a pretty sight. Ultimately however, the native forest will be re-established on the site at a time when natives are becoming ever scarcer.

Gilbert Nature Reserve

Somerset Road, Sandys

The Gilbert Nature Reserve in Sandys is part of the Springfield property. The house was bought by the Historical Monuments Trust in 1966. The adjacent five acres that make up the Gilbert Reserve were purchased by the National Trust in 1973 with the help of the Bermuda Audubon Society and the property owners, Harvey Gilbert and his cousin Gwen DeWolf. They generously reduced the price and gave the Trust plenty of time to pay. Adding the Gilbert Reserve to the Springfield property provided a rare opportunity to reunite a Bermuda manor house with much of its original land. This is especially valuable as both the house and the reserve are open for the public to enjoy.

The nature reserve, half of which is woodland, contains rare examples of some magnificent, mature Bermuda cedars which escaped the cedar scale epidemic, and some of it has been planted with native and endemic trees. The Anita Wingate Trail is named in memory of David Wingate's wife who died in the year the reserve was acquired. The reserve also includes some 2.5 acres of farmland that passing motorists will recognise on the east side of Middle Road in Somerset. These are some of the largest fields in Bermuda, and they are bounded by a Cedar/Palmetto hedge that was planted in 1980 along the southern boundary.

Woodland birds: the Cardinal...

... and the Gray Catbird

The Anita Wingate Trail at Gilbert

KCB

Ancient endemics, the Bermuda Palmetto and Bermuda Cedar, at Gilbert Nature Reserve

Coastline and Islands

RWG

Longtails nest in shoreline cliffs

KCB

Smith's Island

The Trust protects islands and coastline for their environmental value — islands serve as refuges for native species, coastal mangroves are intensely rich ecosystems and coastal cliffs provide nesting areas for the Longtail. But they are important to humans too. Every uninhabited offshore island and undeveloped stretch of coastline creates a sense of space and openness in crowded Bermuda.

Smith's Island Nature Reserve

Smith's Island, 61 acres sitting between St David's and Paget Islands, goes right back to the beginning of Bermuda's story. It was home to the island's three original residents — Christopher Carter, Robert Waters and Edward Chard — the sailors left behind (with the ship's dog) when the rest of the crew left Bermuda for Virginia on the *Patience* and *Deliverance* in 1610. It was the seat of the first government when Bermuda was settled in 1612. Over the years it has been the location of an agricultural station, a whaling station, a smallpox quarantine camp and a plant nursery.

With all its history, Smith's Island remains almost undeveloped today. The eastern third of the island is a National Park. The central section was subdivided into half-acre lots, of which the Trust owns ten, with an unpaved road system. In 1999 the Trust bought the entire western third of the island from the Bourne estate, using the Open Space Fund created by the Bank of Bermuda Foundation, but the fund fell short of the purchase price so Government helped, becoming joint owners of the property with the Trust on the understanding that it would be managed by the Trust and be declared inalienable under the Bermuda National Trust Act. It is also a Nature Reserve under the National Parks Act.

The Bourne land — now called the LA Bourne Nature Reserve — is covered with low-stature thicket, dotted with the bare trunks of the cedar forest killed in the cedar scale epidemic. Cedars are re-growing naturally on the site, and the reserve has a very high percentage of native flora such as Wax Myrtle and Doc Bush, a high survival of mature palmettos, and Bermuda Bedstraw in the ground cover. As a nature reserve, it preserves open space as a remnant of old Bermuda, provides critical habitat and also retains the undeveloped aspect of the islands of St George's Harbour when viewed from the town.

Bee Hive Farm Nature Reserve   Dolly's Bay, St David's

Bee Hive Farm Nature Reserve, the gift of David L White, a former President of the Trust, is a 0.06-acre strip of rocky shoreline along the roadside in St David's on Dolly's Bay. Mr White's grandfather had acquired property in this area over the years 1924-1933, and Mr White gave this piece to the Trust in 1990. According to the deeds, there was a fishpond

The Gull-billed Tern, an uncommon visitor

Bee Hive Farm

Rogue Island

Sisal plants on Saltus Island

Saltus Island

and wooden pier on the site, although neither is in evidence today. Bee Hive Farm Nature Reserve is now covered in Buttonwood and Palmetto and the site is left to nature as one of the shoreline habitats that are becoming rarer with time.

Rogue Island   Ferry Reach, St George's

Named after one-time owner William Rogue, not rogues in general, this fifth of an acre island is located at the western end of Ferry Reach. The heirs of Arthur John Gorham gave the island to the Trust in 1979. Despite its size, it has real environmental importance as one of the few remaining places where Bermuda Bedstraw, a rare endemic plant, can be found. This small island demonstrates the importance of islands, even tiny ones, in the conservation of rare species. The Bermuda Bedstraw was at one time common in the Tucker's Town area, and was harvested in large quantities, dried and used in mattresses. Rogue Island was the second island to be given to the Trust and the Trust was delighted to find the Bedstraw on it. They used this tiny population as a source of seed for re-colonising on Nonsuch Island and other reserves.

Saltus Island Nature Reserve   Soncy Bay, Hamilton Harbour, Pembroke

At 3.2 acres, Saltus Island is one of the larger islands in Hamilton Harbour near Point Shares in Pembroke, and was the first island given to the Trust. It was earlier known as Stowe's Island but was given its current name following its acquisition in 1876 by Samuel Saltus, the founder of the Saltus Grammar School. Given to the Trust by Richard Aeschliman in 1978, the island is to be kept as a nature reserve with no development and no public access. However, due to a problem with invasive species the donor gave permission for a management programme for their removal. The challenging task was taken up by the students of Saltus Grammar School. Funded by a grant from the UK's Overseas Territories Environment Programme, they visit the island regularly to help remove invasives and plant native trees. Their initial focus has been on the casuarinas in the southeastern section of the island which are of the 'walking' variety and spread easily over rock and shallow soil. In 2002 a small patch of the highly endangered Bermuda Bedstraw was discovered, making preservation of native species on this island all the more important.

Buck Island   Little Sound, Southampton

Nicholas Dill and his family wanted to ensure that this four-acre island in Evan's Bay between Jennings and Frank's Bays — part of the natural landscape of the shoreline of Little Sound — would be protected from development. In 2008, after exploring a variety of options, they decided to give it to the Trust, with the Trust leasing it back to the family for 999 years, with protective covenants to ensure that it remains pristine. The Trust has used long leases as a means of protecting historic properties for many years, but this was the first time one was used to protect open space. The island is covered in low scrub, predominantly invasive species, but surrounded by very shallow water in which the Great Blue Heron and Egret wade and feed, and Merganser ducks paddle and dive among them.

RWG

The Great Blue Heron in flight

KCB

Saltus Island

KCB

Buck Island

Marjorie Jackson Nature Reserve
West Side Road, Sandys

Marjorie Jackson came to Bermuda after the Second World War and was employed by the Shell Oil Company all her working life. After retirement she moved to Sandys Parish, contributing energetically to the local community, running a thrift shop called the Bargain Box to support the District Nurse and other local charities. She had no family so she left her small cottage and a separate waterfront lot to the Trust when she died in 2001. The cottage was modern with no historic value, but the land was a beautiful wooded hillside dropping steeply to a small cove in Methelin Bay. The Trust culled the large casuarinas on the sea side and plans to install longtail igloo nests on the offshore stacks where the nesting birds will be protected from cats and dogs. The cottage itself was used to generate rental income to support the Trust's operating funds, and in 2007 it was sold to raise the funds needed to restore Palmetto House.

Morgan's & Palm Islands
Ely's Harbour Sandys

Morgan's and Palm Islands, which can be seen across Ely's Harbour from the Scaur Lodge Nature Reserve, were donated to the Trust in 1983 by the heirs of Fitch Ingersoll, a flamboyant American politician who once challenged John F Kennedy for his Senate seat. Morgan's Island is just over four acres and features a remnant of Bermuda's original native forest containing White Stopper, Jamaican Dogwood and Foresteria. Palm Island is small, just an acre, but it is vitally important as habitat for Bermuda's endemic and highly endangered Skink. The Pembroke Rotary Club carried out a reforestation programme there in the 1990s. Both islands have large populations of nesting Longtails.

The islands are easily accessible by boat, their small sandy beaches making them popular with boaters. However, parts of Morgan's Island are covered with poison ivy, so exploration is not encouraged. Members of the Trust may be granted a licence to camp on Palm Island, and are required to take the greatest care not to harm the Skinks.

KCB

Marjorie Jackson Reserve

Palm Island

KCB

Morgan's Island

Farmlands

The Trust protects farmlands because they are vital to the environment, are an important visual amenity and contribute to both healthy living in Bermuda and economic diversification. In 2002 it was calculated that there were about 380 acres being commercially farmed in Bermuda. A very small percentage of these lands is owned by the farmers themselves, with the vast majority being leased. The Trust leases out about 30 acres of arable land to commercial farmers all over Bermuda, so the Trust has the care of nearly 10% of the total.

Stokes Point Farm Nature Reserve   Mullet Bay Road, St George's

Nea Smith, a long-time supporter of the National Trust, gave her half interest in this eight-acre property to the Trust and with it came the proud farming tradition of her family. Her father Reeve Smith and uncle Howard Smith had originally farmed together in St David's, but they were relocated by the Government when the airport was built. Howard took over Longfield Farm and was also the keeper of the St David's Lighthouse. He became famous for the cultivation of Easter lilies, and is remembered as the man who developed the early-blooming Easter Lily that is named after him, *Lillium howardii*.

In 1941, Reeve Smith purchased Stokes Point Farm from the Government. The house was once a home for nurses who worked at the Sanatorium situated in what is now the main building of the Bermuda Institute of Ocean Sciences.

Over the years, Stokes Point Farm has produced potatoes, onions and celery, and Easter lilies for the New York market. In their day, the Smith brothers were well-known figures in Bermuda, respected as farmers with a flair for the introduction of new and more productive ways of farming and for contributing to Bermuda farming in general.

The property reaches the coastline on both sides, being bounded by a sizeable mangrove swamp at Ferry Reach and on the other side by Mullet Bay. The neighbouring two acres were acquired in 1980 by the Bermuda Audubon Society, which excavated and landscaped Bartram's Pond, opening the property as a nature reserve in 1985.

The area owned by the Trust includes three buildings and several arable fields. The oldest sections of the main house, with their handsome chimneys, are probably more than 200 years old. A gracious Victorian addition now forms the front portion, with its sweeping verandah and welcoming arms steps. The outbuildings, Stokes Barn and Stokes Mews, have been converted into apartments.

The arable field at Gilbert Nature Reserve

Stokes Point Farm

Locust Hall Farm

Middle Road, Devonshire

Locust Hall Farm, 24 acres comprising 12 acres of working farmland and an equal amount of woodland, is one of the largest farms in Bermuda. Edmund Gibbons bought the property in 1970 as he was disturbed about nearby farmland being developed. In 1989 his three children gave the farm to the Trust with the proviso that the arable land be retained as a working farm and that the remaining land be retained as open space and in its natural state. Of the 24 acres, 19 were a gift outright in memory of Edmund and Winifred Gibbons by their children E Graham Gibbons, Sir David Gibbons and Mary Patricia Gibbons Phillips. The remaining five acres were purchased from the Gibbons family trust.

The fields, which are large by Bermuda standards, offer a glimpse of an earlier, rural Bermuda. They are farmed for vegetables and flowers by the Pacheco family. The property also has two cottages and a small Victorian house. In order to fund the purchase of the five acres, the Trust sold a long lease on the Victorian building, which has been renovated. The old Bermuda drystone wall on the southern boundary of the property runs under the shade of the Allspice forest and is covered by the very rare Long Spleenwort Fern.

Paget Marsh Farmland and Lammermuir Cottage

Middle Road, Paget

The acquisition of Paget Marsh involved three parcels of land. The first two were bought in the 1950s by Dr Henry Wilkinson for the Historical Monuments Trust. In 1965, Mary Gray, who owned the third parcel, gave the Bermuda Audubon Society the option to purchase it in her will. Audubon was able to purchase the marshland and the Monuments Trust bought the adjoining farmland and Lammermuir Cottage (once known as Lemon Moor). When the Monuments Trust acquired it, they agreed to a covenant to preserve it as a cottage and farm, which it had been for more than 100 years, as this small advertisement in *The Royal Gazette* of 20 May 20 1851 makes clear:

> "To be let 'Lemon Moor' Cottage, near St Paul's Church, Paget. This is a most conveniently constructed Building, and is well adapted for a GARDENER, from the land about it and its contiguity to Hamilton. It has an excellent Tank, now full of water and from an adjacent Tract of Land, an ample supply of Wood is easily obtainable. The Ground is well enclosed and has on it several productive Sweet Orange, Banana, Pomegranate and other Fruit Trees. An Industrious and Steady Man might either be employed by the Proprietor or take it on his own account."

Other Trust Farmlands

The remainder of the Trust's farmlands are part of other properties described earlier: ten acres at Devonshire Marsh; 2.7 acres at Scaur Lodge; 2.5 acres at the Gilbert Nature Reserve; one acre at Warwick Pond; a quarter-acre at the JMH Cooper Reserve; about an acre at Tivoli; a quarter-acre at Palmetto House; the banana patches at the Butterfield Reserve; the orchard at Elm Lodge; and two acres at Smith's Island. In addition, the Save Open Spaces group manages a nursery at Devonshire Marsh at which they grow endemic plants for use all over Bermuda.

The Eastern Bluebird

Locust Hall Farm

Endemics nursery at Devonshire Marsh

Feral chickens at the Paget Marsh banana patch

KCB

Buy Back Bermuda

The Trust and the Bermuda Audubon Society have enjoyed a fruitful partnership ever since Audubon took a leading role in the creation of the Bermuda National Trust. Early Trust newsletters are full of exhortations to Trust members to support Audubon fund-raising drives. The two organisations own reserves side-by-side in several places, and in some cases like Devonshire Marsh West, they are co-owners. The joint venture Buy Back Bermuda was a natural evolution in this relationship.

Somerset Long Bay East Nature Reserve

Located at the westernmost tip of Bermuda, Somerset Long Bay is perfectly situated to serve as the first landfall for migrating birds from North America. For many years the area was a marshland which would have served the birds well, but in the 1930s the marsh was designated a rubbish dump and eventually filled in with trash. By the 1950s the area was nothing more than a wasteland of bottles, covered by heaps of rubble.

In 1968 Government acquired a central portion of the Long Bay shoreline from the Astwood estate for use as a public beach. A few years later, the Bermuda Audubon Society acquired the portion of beach and filled marshland to the west of the public park. Their chief interest was in restoring the habitat for migrating birds, so they reworked the rubbish fill to create a pond with islands for nesting waterfowl. Local resident Joffre Pitman acquired the filled marshland to the east of the park and, inspired by the reserve created by Audubon, carried out his own pond restoration.

The habitat value of the Audubon and Pitman reserves was greatly enhanced by the fact that they lie on a freshwater lens, so the marshes were essentially freshwater and, with their small islands, excellent habitat

The Green Heron

Somerset Long Bay

Interpretive signage at Pitman's Pond

The Great Egret

Somerset Long Bay

for both resident and migrating birds. In fact, with five resident breeding species, they support more resident breeding waterbirds than any other wetland in Bermuda. So when Mr Pitman decided to sell his property, and the potential buyers wanted to put condominium units or stables on the site, the alarm was sounded and a powerful partnership was born: Buy Back Bermuda.

The Trust and Audubon decided together that when an ecologically significant piece of property was at risk, the fact that the seller needed a commercial price for the land should not be a deterrent, and they believed they could generate the necessary support from the community. Buy Back Bermuda went on to raise the $1.4 million needed for the property, thanks to an enthusiastic response from the public and generous support from the Government, which contributed $300,000 and the fencing for the property. Schoolchildren held fund-raising drives, the business community dug into its pockets and hundreds of individuals contributed to the campaign. This enabled Buy Back not only to purchase the property, but also to carry out extensive improvements including a signposted nature trail and observation bird blind to enhance both the habitat and recreational value of the site. Today Somerset Long Bay is an important wildlife habitat, education and recreation facility, as well as a testament to the Bermuda community's strong desire to retain open space.

Buy Back Bermuda Phase II

In 2007 the second campaign was launched, this time to buy two pieces of property, totalling almost 11 acres. One is a coastal property on the Railway Trail near a public park in Hamilton Parish and the other is hilltop adjacent to a government nature reserve in Southampton, with excellent access potential.

As this book goes to print, the fund-raising goals have almost been met and both the Trust and Audubon look forward to making the same kind of site improvements as were made at Long Bay, enhancing the environmental value of both reserves, creating two sites for recreation and education and continuing this remarkable partnership for the benefit of Bermuda.

Pitman's Pond

The Archaeological Research Committee

Formed 20 years ago the Bermuda National Trust's Archaeological Research Committee (ARC) is a very active volunteer group. Its mission is to undertake archaeological research to gain a better understanding of Bermuda's history and cultural heritage. In addition, committee members conduct emergency rescue digs of properties before they are developed.

The ARC trains local volunteers in the latest archaeological methods by partnering with internationally recognised institutions such as the Colonial Williamsburg Foundation, the University of Bristol and the University of Boston. In addition, committee members work with the Trust's Education Officer to run a summer archaeology camp, 'Time Travellers', to encourage and train the island's budding archaeologists.

The ARC has an Archaeology Lab at Reeve Court in St George's where volunteers clean, document and catalogue each and every artefact recovered from a dig. In addition to providing general archaeological outreach, the committee maintains a permanent exhibit on the archaeology of St George's at Tucker House. In 2005 the ARC organised a major archaeology exhibition with the Bermuda Maritime Museum and the Custodian of Historic Wrecks to celebrate the 500th anniversary of the discovery of Bermuda.

Recent projects have included a Geographic Information System (GIS) survey of the island's heritage sites as well as archaeological research into the early landscape of the town of St George. After excavating at the State House and the first Government House the ARC team is conducting an archaeological survey of St Peter's Church, thereby completing the research of the island's first three public buildings. The ARC will also be taking part in the Bermuda Symposium at the Society for Historical Archaeology's Annual Conference in Toronto 2009.

Excavations

Sandys

Royal Naval Dockyard	1986-87
Springfield, Sandys	2001
Watford Island Cemetery	2004

Pembroke Parish

Government House Gardens	2006

St George's

Tucker House	1997
Reeve Court	1989 & 2003
Stewart Hall	1990-91
Fort Cunningham	1991-92
Old Rectory	1991-92
Bridge House	1993
Mitchell House	1994
Unfinished Church	1994 & 2002
Paget Island	1997
First Government House	2002
Hillcrest and Harbourview	2002
Old State House	2004
St Peter's Church	2008
Whitehall	2008

Smith's Parish

Bailey's Bay Fort	1991
Verdmont	2006 & 2007
Historic Shipyard Survey	2006

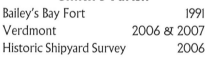
'Time Travellers' working on digs in St George's

CHAPTER 4

COLLECTIONS

W e live at such a feverish pace in our modern world that we sometimes forget that not so long ago craftsmen were still able to work unhurriedly and with a real love of creation. It is important that we should be reminded that we are in danger of losing a heritage of incalculable value. As more is done for the comfort of man, so he seems to become more and more incapable of doing anything for himself. Our world is spinning round too quickly to allow us to think clearly, let alone to create things of eternal beauty.
Eugène Fabergé, Paris, May 1952

The Bermuda National Trust has the awesome responsibility for the care of, and, more importantly, for promoting the understanding and appreciation of a wide range of objects that were crafted here with loving dedication by men and women, both black and white, over the decades.

A Bermuda birds-eye cedar table
by John Henry Jackson c 1849

As the early population settled and became more prosperous, larger stone-built dwellings that were less prone to damage by wind, fire and that pervasive Bermudian dampness, began to evolve. Such homes required furnishings. Bermudians were great travellers and were aware of what was considered stylish in prosperous houses to our north and south. So they brought back ideas. After all, an idea requires little space in the hold of a small ship! They encouraged local carpenters to create furniture based on these ideas, using the wonderful Bermuda cedarwood as a primary timber. Chairs, tables, blanket chests, tallboys and chests of drawers form the bulk of the Trust's collection.

The unsettled state of European affairs during the period 1770-1820 created prosperity for Bermuda's ship owners. By obtaining a licence from the Crown they were able, legally, to hunt for and seize enemy ships. Often the cargos contained silver in various forms. The availability of this raw material led to a creative period for the island's silversmiths both local and visiting. We have, as a result, been left a legacy of simple but beautifully wrought objects.

During the years prior to the invention of the camera, memories were created by skilled people through drawing and painting. The Trust is responsible for an interesting collection of portraits (oils) and for a superb collection of documentary art (watercolours) that depict people, landscapes, seascapes and flora.

Ceramics, glass, metalware and textiles: although most of these things were not crafted locally, each item throws a little light on what life was like on formal occasions and during more intimate times in the reception rooms, the bedrooms, the washrooms and in the kitchens of the Bermudian home.

As we look at these things from our modern perspective, it is worth remembering that most of them were created and manufactured by hand before electricity was discovered.

Trust Collections at the Bermuda Archives

Thomas Driver

The National Trust owns some intriguing and significant elements of Bermuda's heritage in its collection of pictures and documents held at the Bermuda Archives. The collection includes 114 accessioned works, including albums of floral studies and topographic views, and depictions of people and everyday life of years gone by. The Trust's collection which is stored safely in this climate-controlled environment contains a wealth of information on Bermuda's history, including all the deeds for Trust properties.

Thomas Driver

The most important piece in the Trust's Archives collection is a very early map of Bermuda (right) which is attributed to Admiral Sir George Somers. He was the Admiral of the Fleet, travelling on the *Sea Venture* when it wrecked off Bermuda in 1609 on its way to Virginia, marking the beginning of the British settlement of the Somers Isles. Somers and his companions spent nearly ten months in Bermuda, building two small ships, the *Patience* and the *Deliverance*, in which they completed their voyage to Virginia. Somers returned to Bermuda to gather fresh supplies and died here in 1610. His heart is buried in Bermuda and his body was sent back to his home in England. The map is remarkable for its detail and accuracy, and for the tiny image of two men hunting wild hogs with the ship's dog.

The map was acquired by the Historical Monuments Trust in 1948. In his report *The First Thirty Years*, Hereward Watlington described the map as "a map of Bermuda on vellum, which came from the collection of the first Baron Dartmouth, 1648, and bore the Harington Arms. Straechy had presented a manuscript map made by Sir George Somers to Lucy, Countess of Bedford (nee Lucy Harington)". Presumably the Straechy he referred to was secretary-elect of the Virginia colony William Strachey, a passenger on the *Sea Venture*. His account of the shipwreck was said to have been the basis for William Shakespeare's 1611 play *The Tempest*. An original map of Bermuda drawn by the founder of the Bermuda colony was a treasure indeed, and its acquisition was a triumph for the Monuments Trust.

Thomas Driver

The Trust's collection of watercolours by Thomas Driver (details left) have found their way into a number of the books in the *Bermuda's Architectural Heritage* series. His work – accurate depictions of places and buildings – forms an invaluable architectural record of Bermuda in the days he was here, 1814–1836. Driver was an Englishman who came to Bermuda to work as the assistant to the Agent for Victualling His Majesty's Ships at the height of the War of 1812. Driver painted prolifically, using a *camera lucida* (a device which projects an image onto the page) and this accounts for the accuracy of his drawings. After the war he remained in Bermuda working as an auctioneer and continuing to paint.

Edmund Hallewell

Another important piece in the collection is a book of 13 prints by Lieutenant Edmund Hallewell. He came to Bermuda as an ensign in 1841 and within three years had been promoted to adjutant of the 20th Regiment. He later served with distinction in the Crimea and ended his career as the Commandant of the Royal Military College at Sandhurst. In Bermuda he served Governor William Reid and married his daughter. Reid was a notably effective governor, promoting agriculture which had been much neglected and carrying out many other modernising reforms; Reid Street bears his name. Hallewell painted panoramas of the island in watercolours, which were then translated into lithographs and made into the book which the Trust now preserves in the Archives (bottom right and detail left).

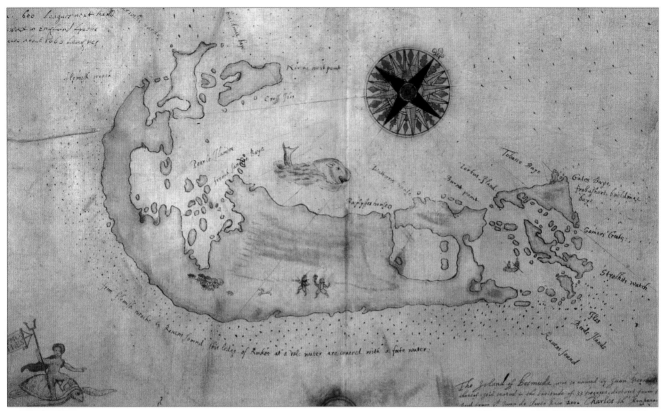

Edmund Hallewell

Lady Lefroy

Lady Lefroy

Edward James

The London printers took considerable liberties with Hallewell's original watercolours, making them more to the fashionable London taste and less accurate in their depiction of Bermuda. Nevertheless, they are beautiful and evocative.

A very different type of character from Driver and Hallewell was another English artist, Edward James. He arrived in Bermuda in 1861 when his ship, bound for New York, called at Bermuda in distress. Having arrived accidentally, he stayed for the rest of his life, dying in Bermuda in 1877. He was a great friend of the US Consul Charles Allen, who represented the Union during the American Civil War. Allen commissioned James to do detailed and accurate paintings of the ships which ran the Union blockade of the Confederate states, many of which called in to Bermuda to collect supplies needed by the Confederacy. Allen sent these to Union Navy commanders to help them intercept the blockade runners, and then James sold copies of the paintings to captains and crews of the blockade runners themselves. James was an alcoholic, and staggered from one job to another, using his skills as a painter to fund his drinking habit. Allen wrote of his friend at one point: "The Devil has full possession of James — he is drunk all the time — I would gladly help him if he would quit drinking, but I fear he never will do." It seems Allen was right. The latest addition to the Trust's collection of James paintings is the magnificent *Confederate Side-wheel Blockade Runner* (right), given to the Trust by Mrs Elfrida Chappell.

Along with the rather grand paintings of the military and marine artists, the collection includes some more domestic works such as Lady Lefroy's botanical drawings. Sir John Lefroy, Governor of Bermuda, 1871-1877, was a well-known scientist whose speciality was the study of magnetism. In Bermuda he took a great interest in the natural environment and produced a compilation of Bermuda's colonial records, published as *Memorials of the Discovery and Early Settlement of the Bermudas or Somer Islands, 1511-1687*. His second wife was an artist with an interest in botany and the Trust's collection contains an album of her illustrations — 80 pictures of exotic flowers with a charming cover (left, top two).

Paintings and Artwork

The National Trust also has a considerable collection of paintings and artwork held outside the Archives; these are an important part of the Trust's collections. Most valued are those painted in Bermuda, especially the Verdmont paintings which are so closely connected to the Trust. There are some 400 pieces in the collection, including many imported prints that would have hung on the walls of the well-to-do in centuries gone by. The collection can be seen at the three Trust museums and in the Trust headquarters at Waterville, while a notable portrait of the Earl of Pembroke hangs in the Cabinet Building.

One of the Trust's treasured possessions is a watercolour of Waterville painted by Bessie Gray in 1896 (right). Born in 1854, she was the daughter of Chief Justice Brownlow Gray. The first known works by Bermuda-born artists date from the 1870s and 1880s and were by Susan Frith, Bessie Gray and the Tucker sisters, Ethel and Kate. Bessie Gray was best known for her appealing renditions of Bermuda flora and old style cottages, but she also dabbled in coastal scenes. The Trust has a newer connection to Bessie Gray: she was the great-great-aunt of the Trust's current Executive Director, Jennifer Gray.

⋏ Edward James

⋎ Bessie Gray

B. GRAY
1896.

△ John Green's Polly

▽ Bruere by John Russell

The Green portraits on display at Verdmont were acquired by Hereward Watlington and made available to the Monuments Trust when they bought Verdmont. John Green, the painter, lived at Verdmont with his wife Mary (known as Polly) and her family from about 1775 until his death in 1802 (see page 34). He came to Bermuda from Philadelphia in the mid 1760s to work as a painter and fell in love with Polly Smith, who was eventually to inherit Verdmont. In 1774 he travelled to London to study painting with his friend, the eminent painter Benjamin West. While in London, he wrote a touching letter to Polly's father, Thomas Smith, in which he despaired of finding the money he needed to marry, spoke of his fiancée as his "dearest treasure" and seemed to be on the most affectionate terms with his future father-in-law. It is thought that after his marriage he contributed greatly to the project of bringing Verdmont into the latest style; it is clear from the letter that Smith and Green shared an interest in art and modern architectural trends.

Green painted all four of Smith's daughters. The most appealing are the portraits of his wife – one of her as a girl (left), one romantic painting of her with her young nephew, and a portrait of Polly as a mature woman (near right). Jokingly renamed by a Trust volunteer as 'Mrs Green with a Headache', it is in fact a lovely study of his wife, a tribute to the affectionate nature of their marriage. He also painted Polly's unmarried sister Honora 'Peggy' twice, once as a girl and again as a mature woman. Polly's sister Elizabeth married Henry Trott (far right) and Green painted both of them; her sister Catherine married Joseph Packwood, and Green painted her and her son.

The Blackburn portraits at Tucker House provide more fine examples of Bermuda's 18th century paintings. Joseph Blackburn was the first portrait painter to visit Bermuda from London, arriving in 1752 and staying for two years. He painted lace and other details of dress with great care and flair and was said to be very flattering to his subjects. It immediately became fashionable to have him paint your portrait if you were a Bermudian of a certain class. While he was in Bermuda he painted at least 25 portraits, after which he went on to a similar social success in Boston. The Trust has examples of his work on display at both Tucker House and Verdmont.

The Tucker House portraits were part of the gift of Tucker furniture and silver, left to the Trust by the will of Robert Tucker of Baltimore (see page 5). In the Tucker House dining room are Blackburn portraits of Frances Tucker (see page 133) and Thomas Tudor Tucker, and in the drawing room are Colonel Henry Tucker (right) and his wife Anne with two of their six children (far right).

At Tucker House there is also a portrait of Governor George Bruere (left) who served in Bermuda from 1764 to his death in 1780. The portrait had remained in the Bruere family until it came up for auction in 2005, and past Trust President David L White bought it for the Trust. Christie's, the auction house, attribute the painting to John Russell, RA, a leading portrait painter of his day in London. Despite his daughter having married into the Tucker family, Governor Bruere fell out irrevocably with Colonel Henry Tucker over the Colonel's negotiations with the American revolutionaries and the open support of two of the other Tucker sons for the American cause, and harsh words were said to have been exchanged. It was felt that it would not be right to hang their portraits in the same room, so Bruere can be found in the bedchamber.

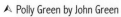 Polly Green by John Green   ⌄ Colonel Tucker by Joseph Blackburn   ⌃ Henry Trott by John Green   ⌄ Mrs Tucker and children by Joseph Blackburn

Furniture

The definitive book on Bermudian furniture and silver is Bryden B Hyde's *Bermuda's Antique Furniture & Silver*, published in 1971 by the newly formed Bermuda National Trust. Furniture was made of the indigenous Bermuda cedar in the earliest days, in styles influenced by English, Spanish and American craftsmen. Hyde described its virtues in cabinetry: "Cedar resists moth, cockroach, cricket, termite and mildew. It is strong and springy, does not warp, is easily worked, turned, carved, and finishes a red colour which fades to honey in sunlight. Its sweet smell is retained for centuries." He believed that the best cedar furniture was made between 1612 and 1750, after which mahogany came into fashion. He considered that the cedar chest-on-frame was the most characteristic of all Bermuda-made furniture, and the most Bermudian feature of these chests was the elaborate chest-front dovetailing.

The Trust's collection includes some 520 pieces, and can be seen at Waterville, Tucker House and Verdmont. Among the earliest are two pieces at Verdmont: a wainscot chair dating from c 1660 and an outstanding Bermuda cedar tallboy which dates from c 1680. In the collection are many first-rate Bermuda-made pieces. The vast majority of the early pieces were probably made by slaves, who were known to be skilled shipwrights, masons, cabinet-makers and silversmiths, as well as fearless and skilled seamen and navigators.

One of the finest pieces in the collection is a cedar tea table c 1740 at Tucker House with dimple knees (described by Hyde as "an incised, pinched, apple-leaf knee"). The design is thought to have been inspired by William Savery, a highly-regarded Philadelphia cabinetmaker who is believed to have visited Bermuda for a short while.

A Queen Anne cedar day bed, c 1740, donated by Trust Patrons Nicholas and Bitten Dill, was described by Hyde as unique and one of the finest pieces of Bermudian furniture in existence. Nonetheless, it has its whimsical aspects: its feet seem to march in different directions. The "split splat" seat back creates mirror images of the silhouette of a parrot's head. This "split splat parrot-back" is also featured in two Queen Anne chairs downstairs at Verdmont.

Much earlier, but equally elegant, are the Trust's cedar high-back chairs, the style which immediately preceded the Queen Anne chairs. There are several at Verdmont including, very unusually, a complete set of six. A pair of smaller ones can be seen at Tucker House. These Bermuda cedar high-back chairs date from the early 1700s. The front stretchers, known as yoke-front stretchers, are flat rather than turned, and they curve upwards. Chippendale chairs succeeded the Queen Anne style and persisted into the early 19th century. They are characterised by the elaborately pierced splat. Although they can have cabriole front legs like the Queen Anne chairs, in most Bermudian examples the front legs are simple and square.

Bryden Hyde's fondness for the cedar chest-on-frame is shared by many Bermudians to this day. The Trust collection includes some 14 of these chests. One of them, left to the Trust by Gloria Higgs as part of the Tivoli collection (shown on page 126), had been in her family since the late 1800s. Now on display at Verdmont this is a classic late 17th century Bermuda chest with crisply turned onion feet, simple mouldings and a gracefully scalloped

Top – a cedar high-back chair with knob finials, c 1680-1740 from Tucker House. Middle – a cedar Queen Anne chair c 1730-1770, with cabriole legs and a slotted or 'split' splat from Verdmont. Bottom – a cedar Chippendale chair with straight legs and a front stretcher, c 1760-1820 at Verdmont.

Top left– a cedar tallboy in the 'William and Mary' style, dating from c 1680, with characteristic 'cupped' legs, from Verdmont. Bottom left– a cedar wainscot chair, c 1660, from Verdmont. These were the earliest chairs made in Bermuda, and this example, in common with most Bermudian chairs in this style, is massive and undecorated. Top right– A cedar table with a mahogany top, c 1670, from Verdmont. Described by Bryden Hyde as "at the pinnacle of this very pleasing style", it shows the typically Bermudian inverted wave motif on the front apron. Middle right– a cedar tea-table from Tucker House, c 1740, with trifid feet and pinched, apple-leaf carving on the knees of the cabriole legs. It has a raised rim to prevent expensive china cups from falling off. Bottom right– a cedar Queen Anne day bed, c 1740, now in Verdmont.

skirt. One telltale sign of early cedar furniture is the size of the cedar timbers from which they were made. On Miss Higgs' chest, the sides and the hinged top are each made of single boards.

Two of the most prominent housewrights and cabinetmakers in Bermuda were the Smith brothers from Paget, Samuel and Henry Smith, who worked with their skilled slaves, Nokey and Augustus. Their workshop produced some of the most sophisticated and elegant furniture ever made here, and the Trust has three outstanding pieces on display at Tucker House: a mahogany desk in the bedchamber, a mahogany chest of drawers donated by Ann Smith-Gordon in the nursery, and a spectacular mahogany roll-top secretaire and bookcase in the library. All three of these pieces display the Smith brothers' signature fluted quarter side-columns.

Finally, there is a small table at Verdmont with a special Trust connection. It is a birds-eye cedar table (pictured on page 117) made by John Henry Jackson for the Great Exhibition of 1851 at the Crystal Palace in Hyde Park, London. This beautiful piece was donated to the Trust by the Jackson family; Wayne Jackson was President of the Trust Council (2001-2004).

Silver

Silver has always been prized both for its aesthetic and functional value and, in the days before modern banking, as a means of providing ready capital when needed. The Trust's collection of some 340 pieces includes items made in England, America and Bermuda. Between 1650 and 1900, 38 silversmiths worked in Bermuda, 12 of them born in the island, at least seven of whom trained abroad. This gave Bermuda-made silver pieces an international flavour, although the North American silversmiths definitely had the greatest influence.

Mrs Allan Smith, to whom Bryden Hyde dedicated his *Bermuda's Antique Furniture & Silver,* wrote the seminal work on Bermuda-made silver in 1945. Called 'Bermuda Silversmiths and Their Silver', it was published in two issues of the *Bermuda Historical Quarterly*. She noted that "while some pieces are not as perfect as others, they are all lovely, satisfying to the eye, and eminently practical for use". To ply their craft, local silversmiths would have melted down the large quantity of silver coin, dishes and old silver in lumps and bars that Bermuda's thriving privateer industry procured in the 18th century wars between England and France.

The 17th century cedar chest from Tivoli, now in Verdmont

The mahogany roll-top secretaire and bookcase from the workshop of Bermudian brothers Samuel and Henry Smith (1770-1837) on display at Tucker House.

Although Bermudian silversmiths made everything from buckles to tea-pots, perhaps the most commonly owned silver articles were spoons. Families would have a few spoons of various sizes and use them interchangeably; it was not until the 19th century that serving spoons, soup spoons, dessert spoons and teaspoons were standardised.

One Bermudian silversmith with a special link to the Trust was Joseph Gwynn, a one-time owner of the Trust's historic property the Casino (see page 10). Gwynn is the man who murdered a neighbour by mistake and was hanged in St George's. Mrs Smith gives a sympathetic telling of the story, perhaps because she admired his work so much. She says he "was a good workman. All of his pieces are of elegant shape and when any ornamentation is used it is simple and of good design and the engraving of initial letters is particularly fine". Rather than being an "ignorant and vicious character" as others thought him, she felt that he was nervous and excitable, although possibly "deranged". His son was also a silversmith, but after the family tragedy, he went to live in the States. The Trust has five of Gwynn's spoons in the collection. Uniquely, he used his initials as his mark and also stamped 'BERMUDA' on some of his pieces, as he did on one of the spoons at Verdmont.

Although most Bermuda-made silver was small-work such as spoons and buttons, one silversmith who worked on larger pieces was Peter Pallais. He advertised in the *Gazette* in 1792:

> "Peter Pallais gold and silversmith in St George's, begs to acquaint the Ladies and Gentlemen of Bermuda that since the death of Mr Thos B Blatchley he carries on (at the same place) the above business in an extensive line. Particularly all kinds of coffee-pots, tankards, silver dishes, milk-pots, soup and punch ladles, spoons etc and every kind of gold and silver work, in the neatest manner, on the most reasonable terms."

One of the milk-pots to which he refers may be the elegant little helmet cream jug pictured right.

Pallais was a close ally of the first Methodist missionary in Bermuda, the Irishman John Stephenson. Stephenson had arrived in Bermuda in 1799 to a storm of protest because many feared that, as an Irishman, he would stir up unrest in the slave population, which is exactly what he did. A law was hastily passed to prohibit preaching by anyone not of the Churches of England or Scotland. In defiance, Stephenson preached at the home of Peter Pallais and both men were arrested. Mrs Smith reports that Stephenson then preached to a crowd through the bars of his gaol cell. Pallais was held for nine days and then released because of ill health. Stephenson was gaoled for six months and left Bermuda the following year. One of Pallais' spoons is pictured right.

The ancient craft of silversmithing is still alive in Bermuda today. Modern silversmiths make objects as beautiful as any in the collection, as demonstrated by the heavy silver box (right) made by David Morrell. He trained in England and worked at Triminghams' department store for 27 years, ultimately becoming the manager of the jewellery workshop. In 1995 he was commissioned by the Trust to make six of the boxes, sporting its palmetto emblem, as gifts for major donors to the *In Trust for All* capital fund-raising campaign. The campaign raised more than $5 million, enabling the Trust to restore historic properties, set up an education programme and purchase open space.

A fine spoon by the St. George's silversmith, Joseph Gwynn (1783-1826), bearing his initials and the mark 'BERMUDA', which only he used.

Top left – a late 18th century silver cream jug by Peter Pallais, in his signature helmet style. Top right – a round-ended silver spoon, by Peter Pallais. Bottom – this silver box with a palmetto (the emblem of the National Trust) in a roundel on the lid is the work of modern-day silversmith David Morell.

Porcelain and Pottery

The Trust has a vast collection of some 870 individual pieces on display at the museums and virtually all imported from England, China or Japan. The pieces mainly date from the 18th and 19th centuries, and reflect the changing tastes and fortunes of their owners during this period.

On display at Verdmont is a blue and gold coffee and tea service, which comes with its own personal legend: it is said to have been a gift for US President Thomas Madison from Napoleon which was intercepted by a local privateer in 1815. The set, which is extensive, is decorated with enameled vignettes in the neo-classical taste popular at the time and each piece is different. It was purchased at an auction of the estate of Miss Bessie Trimingham by Hereward Watlington, and donated to the Bermuda National Trust in memory of Miss Trimingham, who is remembered as one of Bermuda's finest poets and geneaologists.

A much less formal tea service is a floral Coalport service, dating from 1830 and on display in the same cabinet. It was owned by Anna Maria Outerbridge, a well-known suffragist and champion of the Boer prisoners of war. It was left to CO Cooper who gave it to the Trust in memory of Miss Outerbridge. One of the most popular sets of porcelain is the grapevine service at Verdmont. It is Spode of about 1820 with a very unusual pattern rarely seen today.

A favourite with visitors to Tucker House is the colourful 'parrot' set displayed in the dining-room. It is English transfer-printed stoneware, onto which the colours have been added by hand before firing, and dates from c 1840. The pattern was apparently popular at the time, as this set is a compilation from three separate households. In the library there is a large and spectacular Chinese punch-bowl, c 1785, decorated in the *famille rose* palette of colours with a domestic scene and landscapes. Such pieces are known as 'export' or 'trade' porcelain, as they were made in China for the western market and are designed to appeal to contemporary European tastes.

Four cups from the 'Napoleon service'

Even broken and discarded pottery can tell a story. Much of what we know about Bermuda's early days is a result of the work of the Trust's Archaeological Research Committee. Starting in 1988 and working with a group from Colonial Williamsburg, they carried out parallel studies of the homes of Henry Tucker in St. George's and his brother St. George Tucker who had emigrated to Williamsburg in Virginia. The dig at Tucker House revealed a great deal about the life of that family during the time of the American Revolution. Archaeologists found large quantities of stylish and expensive ceramics from England and Continental Europe. The quality of the wares and the existence of matched sets suggests that the Tuckers were an affluent family. Comparisons with Williamsburg artefacts of the same period (1775-1807) show a far greater range of types in Bermuda and suggests that Bermuda with its excellent location for trade, had easier and earlier access to imported goods; for example, many English bone china sherds were found in the cellar. Given that Josiah Spode only perfected the formula for bone china in 1797, it does seem that the Bermuda Tuckers were up to date with the latest London fashions in dinnerware at least. In Williamsburg however, bone china did not appear until after 1830, perhaps reflecting strained trading relations between Britain and the break-away American colonies.

Top — a plate and tureen from the much-loved parrot set displayed on the dining table at Tucker House. Middle left— a jug from the floral Coalport service displayed at Verdmont. Middle right— a dish from the grapevine service at Verdmont. Bottom— this large punch-bowl from Tucker House is a splendid example of late 18th century Chinese export porcelain, made for the western market.

Other Elements of the Collections

The Trust collections also include textiles, books, glassware, tools, household implements and toys, most of which are on display at the Trust museums, and which help to draw a picture of what life at Tucker House or Verdmont would have been like in previous centuries. In the kitchen at Tucker House are household utensils and implements; most notable is the hanging food safe, with its small cup on the chain which would have been filled with oil to deter ants. It came from Verdmont, where Lillian Joell lived without electricity or piped water until 1950, and it probably saw use into the middle of the 20th century.

Another interesting artefact is the collection of brass weights and measures which was once the property of the Smith's Parish Vestry which, in years gone by, was responsible for checking volumes given by parish traders to their customers. These were the master set to which all others had to conform.

The Trust's collection of textiles totals about 400 pieces, many of which are in climate-controlled storage. At the museums are displayed bed-linens, samplers and clothing such as christening gowns. A favourite piece is a wedding dress thought to have been made in Bermuda in the 1850s. It is made of Irish linen decorated with a variety of handwork including broderie anglaise, reticello, French hand sewing and Irish crochet. Torn and crumpled in a brown paper bag, it was given to the Trust's Education Officer to be used in school programmes. She quickly realised that it was much too fine for such purposes and it eventually found its way to Mrs Sally Criswell, an American stitch expert and teacher, who spent over 200 hours restoring it to its original condition.

This enchanting portrait of Frances Tucker, the daughter of Colonel Henry Tucker and sister of President of the Council, Henry Tucker, was painted by Joseph Blackburn. Frances was born in 1740, and as Blackburn came to Bermuda for two years from 1752, the portrait must have been painted when she was between 12 and 14 years of age. Not only does it capture the sitter's innocent charm, it also demonstrates Blackburn's mastery of the details of lace and other female finery for which he was known. Frances married a distant cousin, yet another Henry Tucker, of Bridge House at Somerset Bridge, and lived until 1825. She was the great grandmother of the Robert Tucker of Baltimore who left his furniture and portraits to the Trust, much of which will have descended to him from her.

Index

Bold numbers show the main reference(s) to Trust properties and collections. Italicised numbers refer to illustrations and maps. Street and most other place names have not been indexed.

1968 constitution 3, 5, 86
20th Regiment 118
46th Regiment of Foot 64
56th Regiment 64, 68, 70
68th Regiment of Foot 18
Adams, Henry and wife Sophia 30
Adams, John 60
Aeschliman, Richard 104
African Diaspora Heritage Trail 36
Agriculture and agricultural land 78, 88, 94, *98*, 100, 102, 118
Albouy, Francis 48
Allen, Charles, US Consul 120
Allspice 88, 90, 110
American Civil War 18, 26
American Revolution 12, 16, 52, 58, 64, 122, 130
Amity 34
Anita Wingate Trail 100, *100*
Anole lizard *84, 88, 96*
Antelope, HMS 70
Archaeological digs 4, 14, 18, *18*, 116, *116*, 130
Archaeological Research Committee (BNT) 18, **116**, 130
Ardisia 86
Arnell, Jack, Dr 58
Astwood estate 112
Audubon Society, Bermuda 3, 5, 74, 75, 82, 84, 86, 96, 100, 108, 110, 112, 114
Augustus (slave) 126
Bailey, Roger and family 12
Bailey's Bay Fort 116
Ball, Alexander Forbes 10
Ball, George and wife Esther 10
Bananas 92, 110, *111*
Bartram's Pond 108
Basham, Frederick and wife Catherine Tucker 14
Bay House (St David's) 64
Bedstraw, Bermuda 102, 104
Bee Hive Farm Nature Reserve 75, **102-104**, *103*
Belair 7, **48-49**, *48-49*
Bell, Dunbar, Dr 5
Bennett, Governor 12, 26, 30
Bermingham, Andrew 62
Bermuda Archives 3, 118
Bermuda Bedstraw (see Bedstraw, Bermuda)
Bermuda Government 5, 38, 56, 58, 61-62, 75, 78, 80, 102, 108, 112, 114
Bermuda Historical Monuments Trust 3, **5**, 7, 8, 10, 12, 16, 20, 28, 30, 36, 44, 46, 56, 62, 66, 74, 75, 80, 84, 86, 100, 110, 118, 122

Bermuda Library 5, 20, 56
Bermuda Maritime Museum 3, 58, 116
Bermuda National Trust Act 1969 3, 5, 102
Bermuda National Trust Museum 26
Bermuda Perfumery 20
Bermuda's Antique Furniture and Silver 4, 124, 126
Bermuda's Architectural Heritage book series 4, 26, 40, **60**, 118
Bermudian Heritage Museum 22
Bess (slave) 34
Blackburn Place 50
Blackburn, Joseph 18, 122, *123*, *133*
Blatchley, Thos B 128
Blockade (see Union blockade)
Bluck, Laura Cox 84
Bluebirds 84, *99*, 110
Boardwalk 75, *84*, 86
Boaz Island 68, 72
Boer prisoners of war 68, *68*, 70, 130
Boggs, Robert 18
Bone china (see China)
Botanical Gardens 96
Bourne estate 102
Bourne Nature Reserve (see LA Bourne Nature Reserve)
Bourne, John Tory 26
Brackish Pond 80
Brazil pepper 90, 96
Bridge House *7*, **12**, *12-13*, 116
British Admiralty 58, 62, 68
British Army 3, 62, 66, 75
British West Indies Regiment, 4th Battalion 70, *70*
Brooke, Thomas 8
Bruere, Frances (see Tucker, Frances Bruere)
Bruere, George, Governor 16, 18, 122, *122*
Buck Island *75*, **104**, *105*
Buckingham 5, *7*, **8-9**, *8-9*
Buildings maintenance and restoration 7, 8, 10, 14, 20, 22, 24, 26, 28, 30, 32, 36, 38, 40, 42, 56, 128
Buildings Preservation Committee (BNT) 60
Burchall, James and family 30
Burton, Esther (see Smith, Esther Burton)
Burton, Robert, Captain 10
Butterfield Nature Reserve *75*, **92**, *93*, 110
Butterfield, Deborah St George 2
Butterfield, Dudley, Mr and Mrs 92
Butterfield, Jim 68
Butterflies *83, 85, 90, 98*
Butteries 28, 40, *40*, 56, *57*, 98
Buttonwood 104

Buy Back Bermuda 75, **112-115**
Cabinet Office 120
Cahow 74
Captain I[ngham] 40
Cardinal *91, 100*
Carter, Christopher 102
Casino, the *7*, **10-11**, *10-11*, 12, 18, 128
Casuarina *96*, 104, 106
Catbird *91, 100*
Cattail 82
Caves 86, 90
Cedar furniture 117, *117*, 124-126, *124-126*
Cedar Hill 54
Cedar scale epidemic 74, 75, 100, 102
Cedar, Bermuda 82, 84, 86, 88, *92*, 94, 96, *96*, 100, *101*, 102
Cemeteries 3, **61-73**
Cemetery Hill 62, *62-63*, 65
Ceramics 117
Chaplin O'Neill Nature Reserve *75*, **94**, *94*
Chaplin, Charlie 94
Chaplin, Oona O'Neill, Lady 94
Chappell, Elfrida, Mrs 120
Chard, Edward 102
Checkerboard (Spittal Pond) 80
Chick of the Village (see White-eyed Vireo)
China 18, *19*, 130, *130-131*
Chudleigh, Diana 60
Clipper, Rosemary 60
Cluster Cottage *7*, **52-53**, *52-53*
Coast and island reserves **102-107**
Collections of the Bermuda National Trust 5, **117-133**
Colonial Williamsburg Foundation 5, 116, 130
Commissioner's House **58**, *59*
Common Gallinule 82
Commonwealth War Graves Commission 61, 70, 72
Compulsory purchase of land 38, 66
Confederate Agents 26
Confederate Museum 26
Convict Cemetery 61, **70**, *71*
Convict hulks 58, 72
Convicts 58, 68, 70, 72
Cook, Walter, Mr and Mrs 92
Cooper Nature Reserve (see JMH Cooper Nature Reserve)
Cooper, CO 130
Cooper, Elma Winifred 78
Cooper, John Henry Maxwell 78
Court of Vice-Admiralty 12, 36, 44

Cox, John, Sir 84
Criswell, Sally, Mrs 132
Crown Lands Corporation 38
Cruciform buildings 32, 38
Custodian of Historic Wrecks 116
Damselfly *87*
Darling, Leslie 5
Darrell, Eliza Beltt 50
Darrell, Nathaniel, Captain 50
Daughters of Samaria 22
Davenport Cottage 24, *24*
Davenport, John 22, 24
Day, Samuel, Governor 26
Deeds, property, BNT 118
Deliverance 102, 118
Dennis' Walk *84*
Development Applications Board 96
Devonshire Marsh Nature Reserves 3, *75*, **82-84**,
   82-84, 110, *110*, 112
Dew, George and wife Ann 28
DeWolf, Gwen 100
Dickinson, Elizabeth Jr (later Spofferth) 34
Dickinson, John and wife Elizabeth 34
Dickinson, Mary 34
Died at Bermuda 62
Dill, Bayard, Sir 84
Dill, Joseph and wife Frances Russell Wood 42
Dill, Lucius 42
Dill, Nicholas and family 104, 124
Dill, Tom, Lt Colonel and daughters 42
Dinwiddie, Robert 12
Doc Bush 102
Dockyard, Bermuda *7*, 58-59, 68, 70, 72, 116
Documents, historic 3, 5, 118
Doris 70
Dragonfly *87*
Driver, Thomas 118, *118*, 120
Duck Island 46
Ducks *86*, 104
Dumping 76, 82, 86, 88, 112
Durnford, Andrew, Captain 20
Easter lilies 108
Eaves, typical St George's 22
Education programme (BNT) 4, 86, 114, 116,128,
   132
Egrets 76, *83-84*, *86*, 104, *114*
Elm Lodge Nature Reserve 74, *75*, *94*, *95*, 110
End to End committee, Catlin 88
Endemic species 76, 80, *80*, 82, *85*, 86, 88, 90, 92,
   100, *101*, 104, 106, 110, *110*
Endowment funds 7, 75, 88
Esten, John and family 12
Fanny Fox's Cottage *7*, **30-31**, *30-31*
Farming and farm lands 3, 54, 78, 82, 88, 90, 94,
   96, 100, 108-111, *109*

Feiss, Carl, Dr 60
Ferns 82, 84, 88, 90, 110
Ferrar, Nicholas 40
Ferry Point Military Cemetery **64**
Ferry Reach Military Cemetery **64**, *65*
Ffollett, John and wife Jane 12
Fiddlewood 90
Fidelity International 42
Fish, Florence Voorhees 52
Fish, Hamilton 52
Fish, Peter Stuyvesant 52
Fishponds 16, 42, 102
Flemish gables 10, *11*, 16, *16*, 26
Floral studies 118
Folger, Henry 10
Food safe 132, *132*
Forbes, George 10
Foresteria 106
Fort Cunningham 116
Fort Hamilton 66
Fort Langton 66
Fort Prospect 66
Forth, HMS 68
Foster, Ralph 26
Foster, Thomas 10
Fourways 48
Fox, Benjamin (elder) 24
Fox, Benjamin (younger) 30
Fox, Frances (Fanny) Zuill 30
Fox, William Hayward 8
Fraser, Richard and Helen 80
Freesias 78, *78*
Friendly Societies 22
Frith, Hezekiah 94
Frith, John, Dr and wife Emily 54
Frith, Sanders 54
Frith, Susan 120
Fund-raising campaigns and events 4, 7, 20, 76,
   86, 96, 112, 114, 128
Furniture 5, 16, 18, 50, 22, **124-126**
Gallagher, Dr 68
Gambusia 78, 80, 82, 88
Garden Club of Bermuda, the 3, 5
Garrison Cemetery **61-62**, *61-63*
Garrison Cemetery Prospect 61, **66-68**, *67*
Geographic Information System 116
Georgina 46
German prisoners 70
Giant Balloon Vine 92
Gibbons Nature Reserve *75*, **82**, *82*
Gibbons, David, Sir 82, 110
Gibbons, E Graham 82, 110
Gibbons, Edmund and wife Winifred 82, 110
Gibbs Hill Lighthouse 96
Gilbert, Ephraim and wife Mary Hinson 56

Gilbert, Harvey 100
Gilbert, Henry Hunt and daughters 56
Gilbert, Thomas 56
Gilbert Nature Reserve 56, *75*,**100-101**, *101*, *109*,
   110
Glade, the 72
Gladys Morrell Nature Reserve*75*, **98-100**, *98-99*
Glass 18, 117, 132
Global warming 86
Globe Hotel 5, *7*, **26-27**, *26-27*
Goldfinch *96*
Goldsmiths 128
Goodfellow, Adrianna 50, 92
Goodrich, Bridger 12
Goodrich, Elizabeth Tucker 12
Gorham, Arthur John, heirs 104
Gosling and Co 18
Gosling, Alice Emily (Elsie) 46
Government House (1721, now Rectory) 20, 32
Government House (1st) 26, 116
Government House (Pembroke) 116
Gray, Bessie 120, *121*
Gray, Brownlow, Chief Justice 120
Gray, Jennifer 120
Gray, Mary 84, 110
Great Exhibition 126
Green, John 36, 122, *123*
Green, Mary (Polly) Smith 36, 122, *122*, *123*
Green, Mary Jane Mitchell (see Mary Jane Mitchell
   Green Memorial Garden)
Gregg, James, Gunner *68*, 70
Grenadier Guards, 2nd Battalion 62, 72
Guava 86
Gunpowder Plot 16
Gurr, Frank 12
Gwynn, Joseph 10, 128, *128*
Hall, Joyce 60
Hallewell, Edmund G, Lt 118, *118*, *119*, 120
Hamilton, Alexander 52
Handy, Thomas and wife Martha Pearman 24
Harbourview 116
Harmony Hall (Warwick) 50
Harris, Edward, Dr 58
Harvey, Althea 18
Harvey, Benjamin Dickinson 18
Harvey, Samuel Augustus 48
Hay, William 32
Hayward Burial Ground *61*, **64**, *64*
Hayward family 64
Hayward, Anthony 64
Held in Trust 1st edition 1989 1, 2, 4
Heliconia 92
Heron 74, 76, *76-77*, *81*, 104, *105*, *112*
Higgs Nature Reserve 54, *75*, **88**, *88-89*, 96
Higgs, Gloria 54, 88, 96, 124, 126, *126*

Higgs, Stanley 54
Higinbothom, Reginald 10
Hillcrest 116
Hinson, Benjamin 42
Hinson, Cornelius 42
Hinson, Edward 56
Historic buildings 2-4, **7-60**, 75
Historic Buildings Committee (BNT) 60
Historic Buildings Survey (BNT) 60
Historical Monuments Trust (see Bermuda
   Historical Monuments Trust)
Historical Society of Bermuda, the 3, 5
History of Mary Prince, a West Indian Slave, The 40
Holland, Elizabeth 12, 14
Holland, Thomas, Reverend 14
Hollis, Gerald Dupont 78
Hospitals 66, 68, 70, 96
Household implements, utensils and tools 132, *132*
HT North Nature Reserve *75*, **76**, **78**
Hubbard, John, Sheriff 20
Hubbard, Sarah Tucker 16
Hughes Nature Reserve (see IW Hughes Nature
   Reserve)
Hughes, Idwal W, heirs 90
Hunt, Thomas and wife Mary Gilbert 56
Hunt, Thomas II and wife Susannah 56
Hunter, Dr Joseph 10
Hurricane Fabian 50, 72, 80
Hyde, Bryden 4, 124, *125*, 126
Imperial Order of the Daughters of the Empire 98
Inalienability 3, 90, 102
Independent Order of Good Samaritans 22
Ingersoll, Fitch, and heirs 106
Ingham, Benjamin 40
Ingham, John, Captain and wife Mary Spencer
   Albouy 40
International Conference of National Trusts 4
Invasive species 75, 86, 90, 92, 96, 98, 100, 104
Ireland Island 68, 70, 72
Islands 46, 102, 104, 106
Ives, Elsa Beatrice Mott 98
IW Hughes Nature Reserve *75*, **90**, *90*
Jack's Pond 88
Jackson, John Henry *117*, 126
Jackson, Marjorie 106
Jackson, Wayne 126
Jamaican Dogwood 106
James, Edward 120, *120-121*
Jarvis, Michael, Dr 26, 56, 60
Jeffrey's Hole (Spittal Pond) 80
Jehovah's Witnesses 10
Jennings family 66
Jennings Land Burial Ground *61*, 66
JMH Cooper Nature Reserve *75*, **78**, *78*, 110
Joell, Alan Paul 36

Joell, Irene 36
Joell, Lillian 36, 132
Joell, Stafford and wife Emma Spencer 36
John Smith's 1624 map 8
Jones, Conrad and wife Jane Trimingham 44
Jones, Edward, Provost Marshal 30
Jones, Thalia (Tilly) and family 32
Keep Bermuda Beautiful 3, 5
Keep, the 3, *7*, **58-59**, *58-59*
Killifish, Bermuda 76, 88
King George V 62
Kitchener, John, Sergeant 72
Kitchener, Walter, Sir, Governor 68
L'Armide 70
LA Bourne Nature Reserve **102**
Lammermuir Cottage 86, **110**
Lang, William, Lt and wife Martha Hayward 64
Lateral steps 10, 16, *17*, 40
Lefroy, John H, Sir, Governor 4, 120
Lefroy, Lady, botanicals 120, *120*
Lighthouse Hill Nature Reserve *75*, **96-98**, *97*
Lime kiln 94
Lines, David 68
Listing of buildings by the Bermuda Government 7
Lizards *84*, *88, 96*
Lloyd, Margaret 60
Loblein, Christian 54
Loblein, Ernest 54
Locust Hall Farm 3, *75*, **110**, *110*
Long Island Cemetery *61*, **68**, *68-69*, 70, 72
Long leases 7, 10, 24, 42, 48, 52, 104, 110
Longtails 74, *79*, 102, *102*, 106
Loyal Hill 84
Lucas, Elizabeth 20
Madison, Thomas, US President 130
Maintenance of buildings policy 7
Maintenance of nature reserves (see Woodland
   management)
Mangrove Lake 76, *77*, 78, *79*
Mangroves 76, *76*, 78, 86, 102, *103*, 108
Mangroville Cottage **78**, *78*
Maps 5, 8, 118, *119*
Mariners' Cemetery (see Nonsuch Island
   Mariners' Cemetery)
Maritime Museum, Bermuda (see Bermuda
   Maritime Museum)
Marjorie Jackson Nature Reserve *75*, **106**, *106*
Marlberry (see Ardisia)
Marshland 76, 78, 80, 82, 84, 86, 88, 110, 112
Martha 46
Mary Jane Mitchell Green Memorial Garden *45*, 46
Mary Prince 40
Masterworks Foundation 8
Membership and events 4

*Memorials of the Discovery and Early Settlement
   of the Bermuda or Somers Islands* 4, 120
Metalware 117
Methelin Bay 106
Methodism 128
Middleton family 92
Middleton, John 24
Middleton, Rebecca 92
Military Cemetery (see St George's Military
   Cemetery)
Military hospital (Ports Island) 68, 70
Military hospital (Prospect) 68
Mills, Samuel and family 8
Mints 84
Mitchell House 16, 20, 116
Mitchell, James 10
Mitchell, Walter 20
Moore, Thomas 8, 14, *14*
Moorhen 82, *82*
Morgan and Palm Islands Nature Reserve *75*, **106**
Morgan's Island *75*, 98, 106, *106-107*
Morrell, David 128, *129*
Morrell, Gladys 98
Mosquito control 78, 82, 86, 88,
Mosquito fish 78, 80, 82, 88,
Mott, CS, family 98
Mounting blocks 38, *39*, 52
Mowbray, Louis S 74
Mulder, Shirley 50
Murphy, Robert Cushman 74
Napoleon 130, *130*
National Parks 75, 78, 96, 98, 102, 112, 114
National Parks Act 1986 75, 102
Native species 75, 76, *79*, 80, *87*, 90, *91*, 92, 98,
   100, 102, 104
Naturalised species 80, 94,
Nature reserves 7, 66, 75, **76-109**
Nature trails 75, *78*, 84, 88, 94, *98*, 114
Nautilus 12
Naval Quarantine Station 68
Nea 14
Nelmes, Thomas, Captain 94
Nokey (slave) 126
Nonsuch Island 66, *66*, 74, 104
Nonsuch Island Mariners' Cemetery *61*, **66**, *66*
North Nature Reserve (see HT North Nature
   Reserve)
North, Mr and Mrs Henry Thompson, heirs of 76
North, Natalie, Miss 78
Norwood, Richard, Survey 1663 12, 40, 66
O'Neill, Eugene and family 94
Old House Survey (BNT) 60
Old Rectory, the 5, *7*, **28-29**, *28-29*, 116
Olivewood Bark, Bermuda 90
Onions, Wilfred 5, 36, 56

Open Space Committee (BNT) 74
Open Space Fund of the Bank of Bermuda 102
Open space purchase 5, 7, 75, 90, 96, 102, 112-114, 128
Orange Grove 30
Orange Valley 84
Oration Stand 72
Orchards 78, 94, *95*, 110
Outerbridge, Anna Maria, Miss 130
Outerbridge, Rebecca Hubbard 16
Overseas Territories Environment Fund 96, 100, 104
Pacheco family 110
Packwood, Catherine Smith 122
Packwood, Joseph 122
Paget Island 116
Paget Marsh Nature Reserve 3, 5, 74-75, *75*, **84-86**, *84-86*, 88, 110, *111*
Paintings 3, 5, **117-123**
Pallais, Peter 128, *129*
Palm Island *75*, 98, **106**, *106*
Palmetto House 5, *7*, **38-39**, *38-39*, 106, 110
Palmetto, Bermuda 82, *82*, 84, *85*, 86, *91*, 92, *93*, 94, *95*, 96, 100, *101*, 102, 104
Palms 86, *89*, 90, 92
Pasture or grazing 82, 88, 94, 96
Patience 102, 118
Pattison, Pierre and wife Laura Nelmes 94
Pearl 68
Pearman, William 24
Pembroke Hall **42-43**, *42-43*
Pembroke Rotary Club 106
Pembroke, Earl of, portrait 120
Peniston's Pond 80
Phillips, Mary Patricia Gibbons 110
Piracy 34
Pitman, Joffre 112, 114
Pitman's Pond 112, *112-113*
Planning Department 4
Plough 20
Poinciana House 28
Poinciana tree 78
Poison ivy 106
Police Service, Bermuda 66, 68
Porcelain **130-131**, *131*
Portraits 5, 18, 36, 117, 120, **122-123**, *122-123*, *133*
Ports Island Cemetery *61*, **68**, *68*, **70**
Ports Island Hospital 68
Post offices 78, 88
Potter, Margery 24
Pottery **130**
Powell Woodland *75*, **86, 88**, 92, 96
Powell, Graham 86
President Henry Tucker House (see Tucker House)
Prince George, HRH (see King George V)

Prince, Mary 40
Princess Louise Lodge 12 22
Privateering 12, 28, 36, 44, 94, 117, 126
Prospect Garrison 38, 66, 68
Protective covenants 7, 52, 94, 96, 104
Quarantine stations 66, 68, 102
Queen's Royal Regiment, 2nd, 2nd Battalion 62, 64, 72
Railway Trail 88, 92, 98, 114
Rainey, Joseph Hayne 18, *18*
Ramsar Convention and sites 76, 78, 82, 88
Rankin family 12, 26
Rankin, George 12
Rankin, Samuel Crofts 8, 26
Rebecca Middleton Nature Reserve *75*, **92**, *92-93*
Rechab Lodge 22
Reeve Court *7*, 10, 12, **14-15**, *14-15*, 18, 116
Reeve, Thomas and wife Elizabeth Tucker 14
Reformed Episcopal Church 32
Reid, Thomas and wife Frances Dill 42
Reid, William, Governor 118
Requisitioning of land 38, 66
Rich Papers 4
Richards, Dr 68
Richardson, Alexander, Reverend and wife Ann Somersall 28
Richardson, James 18
Robinson, Lydia Moncure 48
Rogue Island *75*, **104**, *104*
Rogue, William 104
Rogues and Runners: Bermuda and the American Civil War 26
Rose Society Repository Garden 44, *44*, 46, *47*
Royal Artillery 62, 70
Royal Bermuda Yacht Club 48
Royal Engineers 20, 60
Royal Marines 68, 72
Royal Naval Cemetery *61*, 68, **72**, *72-73*
Royal Naval Hospital 68
Royal Navy 20, 58, 72
Royal Poinciana 78
Rushes 82
Russell, John, RA 122, *122*
Salt marsh 80
Saltus Grammar School 104
Saltus Island Nature Reserve *75*, **104**, *104-105*
Saltus, Samuel 104
Saltwater ponds 76, 78, 86
Salvation Army Hall 32
Samaritans' Cottages *7*, **24-25**, *24-25*
Samaritans' Lodge *7*, **22-23**, *22-23*, 24
Samson, George Mackenzie, Petty Officer, VC 62, *62*, 64
Sandys Community Centre 56
Savage map 52, 60, *60*, 70

Savage, AJ, Lieutenant 60, *60*, 70
Save Open Spaces fund-raising campaign 76
Save Open Spaces group 110, *110*
Savery, William 124
Sawgrass 82
Sayle, William, Governor 34
Scaur Lodge Nature Reserve *75*, **98**, *98-99*, 106, 110
School Lands Cottages *7*, **40-41**, *40-41*
Sea Venture 118
Seabirds 74, *79*, 102, *102-103*, 106
Seaside Oxeye *94*
Secretary Road 62, 64
Section 34 94, 96,
Sedge 82, 86, 92, *92*
Shaddock Grove 52
Sharpe, John, Sir, and family 88
Sherwin, Dennis 84, 86, 88
S-Hill Land Nature Reserve *75*, **92**
Ship's Inn *7*, **50-51**, *50-51*, 92
Shipyards 116
Shorto, Sylvia 60
Silver 5, 12, 117, 122, 126
Silversmiths 20, 117, 124, 126, 128, *128*
Sisal *104*
Skinks 106
Slavery and slave trading 28, 40
Slaves 34, 36, 40, 52, 80, 124, 126, 128
Smith, Alfred Blackburn and wife 50, 52
Smith, Allan, Mrs 126, 128
Smith, Catherine (see Packwood, Catherine Smith)
Smith, Elizabeth (see Trott, Elizabeth Smith)
Smith, Esther Burton 10
Smith, Honora (Peggy) 122
Smith, Howard 64, 108
Smith, Mary (Polly) (see Green, Mary (Polly) Smith)
Smith, Nea 108
Smith, Reeve 108
Smith, Samuel (of Pembroke) 14
Smith, Samuel and Henry (of Paget) 126, *127*
Smith, Thomas (of the Casino) 10
Smith, Thomas Lea 52
Smith, Thomas, Captain, and wife Effie 16
Smith, Thomas, Collector and wife Elizabeth Spofferth 16, 34, 36, 122
Smith's Island Nature Reserves *75*, **102**, *102*, 110
Smith's Marsh 82
Smith-Gordon, Ann 126
Society for the Prevention of Cruelty to Animals 86
Somers map 118, *119*
Somers, Sir George 84, 118
Somersall, Richard 28
Somerset Long Bay East Nature Reserve *75*, **112-114**, *112-113*
Somerset Island Military Cemetery *61*, **70**, *70-71*

Somerset Long Bay 112, 114
Somerset Rectory (Bridge House) *133*
Spanish Rock 80
Spencer, Rupert Hugh 36
Spider *95*
Spithead 94
Spittal Pond Bird Sanctuary and National Park 3-5, *75*, **78**, *78-79*, 80, *81*
Spode, Josiah 130
Spofferth, Perient and wife Elizabeth Dickinson 34
Springfield 5, *7*, **56-57**, *56-57*, 100, 116
Spurling, Raymond, Dr 24
Spurling, Stanley, Sir 5
St Andrew's Cross 94
St George's Garrison 62
St George's Historical Society 3-5, 20
St George's Military Cemetery *61*, **62**
St Peter's Church 4, 28, 32, 64, 11
State House 5, 8, *9*, 10, *10*, 14, 116
Stephenson, John 128
Steps (see Lateral steps or Welcoming arms steps)
Stewart Hall *7*, **20-21**, *20-21*, 116
Stewart, Duncan 20
Stilt Sandpiper 79
Stokes Point Farm Nature Reserve *75*, **108**, *109*
Stone walls (drystone) *93*, 110
Story of Bermuda, The 46
Stowe's Island 104
Strode, Hudson 46
Terns *103*
Terrapins 76, *79*
Terror, HMS 70
Textiles 117, 132
The Casino (see Casino, the)
The Globe Hotel (see Globe Hotel, the)
The Keep (see Keep, the)
The Old Rectory (see Old Rectory, the)
Thurber, James 46
Tivoli 3, *7*, **54-55**, *54-55*, 88, 96, 110, 124, *126*
Tivoli North Nature Reserve *75*, **96**, *96*
Todd, Henry and William 8
Topographic views 118
Trimingham family 44, 46
Trimingham, Andrew 46, 58, 60
Trimingham, Bessie, Miss 130
Trimingham, James Harvey and wife Charlotte 44
Trimingham, James Harvey II and wives and daughters 44, 46
Triminghams' store 44, 46, 128
Trinity Church (Hamilton) 32
Tropic Bird (see Longtails)
Trott, Elizabeth Smith 122
Trott, Henry 122, *123*
Trott, John 24

Trott, John Henry and wife Harriet Brownlow Hurst 36
Trott, Samuel Henry and wife Sarah Musson 36
Trott, Thaddeus and daughters 66
Trott's Pond 78
Trustworthy shop 4, 26
Tucker family 5, 26
Tucker House 5, *7*, **16-19**, *16-19*, 34, 116, 118, 122, 124, *124*, 125, *127*, 130, *131-132*, 132
Tucker, Aubrey Harvey 18
Tucker, Elizabeth (see Goodrich, Elizabeth Tucker)
Tucker, Elizabeth (later Reeve) 14
Tucker, Ethel and Kate 120
Tucker, Frances (daughter of Col Henry) 18, 122, *133*
Tucker, Frances Bruere 16, 18
Tucker, George 20
Tucker, Henry (of Bridge House) *133*
Tucker, Henry, Colonel, and wife Anne 16, 122, *123*, *133*
Tucker, Henry, President 16, 18, 130, *133*
Tucker, Richard, Dr and wife Mary 14
Tucker, Richard, Reverend 18
Tucker, Robert (of Baltimore) 5, 16, 122
Tucker, St George 16, 130
Tucker, Territt Fraser and wife Sofia 14
Tucker, Thomas Tudor 122
Tucker, William and wife Hester Louise (Nea) 10, 14, 18
Tucker, William Henry, Dr 26
Tucker, William Tudor 18
Tulloch, Hilary and Richard 62, 70
Typhoid 68, 70
Unfinished Church *7*, **32-33**, *32-33*, 116
Union blockade 26, 120
United Nations Educational Scientific Cultural Organisation 60
Verdmont 5, *7*, **34-37**, *34-37*, 116, 120, 122, 124, *124-126*, 128, *130-132*, 132
Victoria Cross 62
Vines 92
Volunteers 3-4, 60, 92, 116
Voorhees, Clark 52
Voting shares 86
Wadson, TJ 54
Walker, Norman, Major 26
Walking trails 75, *78*, *84*, 88, 94, *98*, 114
Walsingham 48
Walsingham formation and stone 58, 90
Walsingham Trust 90
Ware, AM (Mo), Wing Commander and wife Sylvia 38
Warwick Academy students 92
Warwick Pond Nature Reserve 3, 75, *75*, **86-88**, *86-87*, 110
Warwick Riding Stables 88

Warwick West Marsh 88
Watercolour paintings 117-118, *118-119*, 120
Waters, Robert 102
Waterville 5, *7*, **44-47**, *44-47*, 50, 120, *121*, 124
Waterville Park 44, **46**, *46*, *75*
Watford Cemetery 58, *61*, **72**, *72*, 116
Watlington, Hereward 5, 12, 36, 38, 84, 118, 122, 130
Wax Myrtle 82, 102
Wedding dress 132, *132*
Welcoming arms steps 28, *28*, 38, *39*
West End Development Corporation 61
West Indian Topshell 74
West, Benjamin 122
Wetlands 74, 75, **76-89**, *76-89*, 88
Whaling 80, 102
White Hill 66, 68
White Stopper 106
White, David L 18, 60, 102, 122
White, EB 46
White-eyed Vireo 74, *80*, 90, *99*
Whitehall 28, 116
Wigeon Grass 80
Wild Bermuda Pepper 86
Wild Freesias 78, *78*
Wilkinson Nature Reserve **90**
Wilkinson, Edgar Campbell, Dr 40
Wilkinson, Henry Bernard Logier and wife 90
Wilkinson, Henry, Dr 5, 36, 48, 80, 84, 110
Williams, Benjamin S and wife Frances Cox Williams 38
Williams, William 38
Windsor 8
Wingate, Aileen Pattison 94
Wingate, Anita 66, 100
Wingate, David, Dr 5, 66, **74**, *74*, 86, 94, 100
Witchcraft 24
Women's Work Exchange 50
Wood, Richard 42
Woodland management 74, 75, 86, 88, 90, 92, 94, 96, 98, 100, 104
Woodland reserves **90-101**
Woods, Michael 62
World Heritage Site 60
World War I 58, 70
World War II 72, 75, 106
Yellow fever 58, 62, 64, 66, 68, 70, 72
Yellow Fever cemeteries *61*, **64**, *65*
Yellow-crowned Night Heron 74, 76, *77*, *81*, 88
Zuill, Eugenius 84
Zuill, Frances (see Fox, Frances (Fanny) Zuill)
Zuill, Frances Adrianna Smith 50, 52
Zuill, William (brother of Fanny Fox) 30
Zuill, William Edward Sears 5
Zuill, William Sears 3-5